Test Yourself in

COMPANY LAW

Test Yourself in

COMPANY LAW

Catherine Downs
MA (Cantab), PGCE, Solicitor

&

James Kirkbride
LLB (Hons), MPhil, PGCE

Series Editor: Adrian Keane, Barrister,
Reader, ICSL

BLACKSTONE
PRESS LIMITED

First published in Great Britain 1997 by Blackstone Press Limited,
9–15 Aldine Street, London W12 8AW. Telephone: 0181-740 2277

© Catherine Downs and James Kirkbride, 1997

ISBN: 1 85431 629 X

British Library Cataloguing in Publication Data
A CIP catalogue record for this book is available from the British
Library.

Typeset by Style Photosetting Limited, Mayfield, East Sussex
Printed by Bell and Bain Limited, Glasgow

CONTENTS

FOREWORD

The preparation of this book represents the authors' experience of teaching company law to undergraduates, postgraduates and professional students in law, accountancy and business studies. Its contents examine a full range of company law issues from incorporation, management and its control, through to insolvency, mergers and takeovers. It is hoped that the reader finds the questions and contents both challenging and informative.

Catherine Downs
James Kirkbride
May 1997

INTRODUCTION

PLEASE DO NOT ATTEMPT, OR EVEN READ, THE MULTIPLE CHOICE TEST QUESTIONS CONTAINED IN THIS BOOK UNTIL YOU HAVE READ THIS INTRODUCTION!

A. THE PURPOSE OF THE MULTIPLE CHOICE TESTS

It must be rare, on opening a book and turning to its first page to be greeted by a command, albeit a polite command. However, there is a good reason for such a command: that if you do embark upon testing yourself in company law by using the Multiple Choice Tests (MCTs) in this book *before* you have read the following few pages on: (a) the purpose of these MCTs, (b) the nature and format of the MCTs, (c) popular misconceptions and (d) advice on taking the tests, then it is likely that you will simply defeat the purpose of this book.

The MCTs contained in this book have two purposes. The first is to enable you to test, with speed and accuracy, whether you have a sound working knowledge and comprehension of the main principles of law and the leading cases in company law. The MCT questions used are directed at the general rules, the principal exceptions to those rules and the leading authorities. Wherever possible, they concentrate on the modern law and important decisions. They are not directed at narrow, antiquated, abstruse or esoteric decisions that a practitioner, or even a scholar, might need to look up and research. This explains why, as we shall see, each question has to be answered in only $2\frac{1}{2}$ minutes.

The second purpose is to enable you, after the test, to look at the answers which have been provided and to identify, with precision, your weaknesses and the gaps in your knowledge and understanding, so that you can revisit these areas and take appropriate remedial action.

B. THE NATURE AND FORMAT OF THE MCTs

This book contains two MCTs, MCT1 and MCT2, which together cover most subjects normally found in the syllabus for undergraduate courses in company law.

Each of the MCTs comprises 60 questions, to be taken at one sitting. The 60 questions set have to be answered in no more than $2\frac{1}{2}$ hours. This means that if you divide the time equally between the questions, you will have 2 minutes and 30 seconds to answer each question.

Format

The questions in the MCTs contained in this book are always accompanied by four possible answers: [A], [B], [C] and [D]. You are required to select just one answer, the one that you think is correct/the best.

The questions often take the form of a factual problem and conclude with a specific question, such as 'On these facts what is the most appropriate advice to give to the client'? or 'On these facts what is a correct statement of X's rights?' Questions of this kind are designed to test whether you are able to recognise the law appropriate to the given facts and/or whether you are able to apply the law to the facts and thereby identify the correct outcome.

Other questions take the form of a number of legal propositions, only one of which is correct, or as the case may be, incorrect, or they ask about a specific point of law. Thus as to the former, the question may read, 'Which of the following propositions is correct?' or 'Which of the following propositions is INCORRECT?' As to the latter, the question may state a rule of law and then conclude, for example, 'Which of the following is NOT an exception to this general rule?' Questions of this kind are designed to test your knowledge of the law.

Some questions combine both a factual scenario and a choice of legal propositions so that, after setting out the facts, the question may read, for example, 'Which of the following best describes the principles which the court would apply to these facts?'

C. MCTs — POPULAR MISCONCEPTIONS

MCTs are easier than traditional examinations

This view tends to be expressed by those who have never attempted an MCT. Multiple choice tests are not easier — they are different. The experience of students who have taken MCTs, both at home and overseas, is that such tests are, in their own way, much more demanding than traditional examinations. There are three principal reasons for this.

First, MCTs typically cover the whole syllabus. If you have been brought up on conventional examinations and have adopted the 'question-spotting' approach, the MCT will obviously come as a very nasty shock!

Secondly, the MCT offers no scope for the student who would waffle. In conventional examinations, some students, unaware or not too sure of the correct answers, will hedge their bets, setting out at length all such seemingly relevant legal knowledge as they possess, but making no real effort to apply the law, simply skirting around the central issues with deliberate equivocation. There is no scope for such tactics in the MCT: faced with four competing answers, only one of which is correct, you must nail your colours to the mast.

Thirdly, there is the obvious pressure that comes from having to answer 60 questions at the rate of $2\frac{1}{2}$ minutes per question. This calls for the ability to analyse, digest and comprehend material at speed, before reaching a firm conclusion, only to move on to repeat the exercise in the next question, and so on.

MCT means multiple guess

It is perfectly accurate to say that if you attempt an MCT in which each question had four competing answers, then by the law of averages you *can* score 25%. Sensible students, however, do not approach MCTs in the same way that they approach the national lottery. In the real world, even if they did, it would be of little assistance — the passmark in an examination is usually more than double 25%! On the Bar Vocational Course, for example, a student who answers correctly 60% of all the questions set (in the MCT in civil evidence and procedure or criminal evidence and procedure), will achieve a bare pass; and in many jurisdictions the percentage required to pass is much higher. Further information is given below on how to mark and rate your performance in the MCTs in this book.

MCTs are inferior to traditional tests and examinations

The validity of this criticism depends on what one is seeking to test or examine. Obviously the MCT is not an appropriate tool to test oral legal skills such as advocacy or negotiation, just as it would be an inappropriate means of testing the practical skills of a pianist or an airline pilot. Equally, it cannot test your *creative* legal powers, whether in writing a legal essay or answering a legal problem (although it is interesting to note, in passing, that there is a high degree of correlation between student results in MCTs and in other forms of testing which do involve oral performance and creative written work). However, experience shows that the MCT is an excellent vehicle for testing, with accuracy, levels of knowledge and comprehension and the power of legal analysis, in particular the ability to recognise the law appropriate to any given set of facts, to apply that law, and thereby to identify the correct outcome.

MCTs cannot test the grey areas

This is simply incorrect! For every 'grey area' question, there can be a suitably 'grey area' answer. For example, if on a particular point the authorities conflict, the correct answer may simply read, 'The authorities are in conflict on this point'. (Note, however, that such wording may also be used for an incorrect answer, i.e. in a question where the authorities are not in conflict at all.) Another possibility, in 'grey areas', is to build a question around the facts of an important reported case, thereby testing whether you know of, and have understood, that case. That said, it is certainly true that it can be more demanding to set good MCT questions on 'grey areas', and for this reason they tend to be avoided, unless they concern an important area of the law.

D. ADVICE ON TAKING THE TESTS

The purpose of the MCTs in this book is likely to be defeated unless you observe certain basic rules.

1. *Do not attempt an MCT until you have completed your studies in the subjects covered*

The MCTs in this book are designed to be taken only *after* you have completed your studies in the subject areas covered by the MCT in question and *before* you are formally examined in them.

2. *Take the MCT under examination conditions*

Make sure that you will have an *uninterrupted* period of $2\frac{1}{2}$ hours in which to complete *the whole test*. Also, remove from the room any relevant books or materials that you might be tempted to use — the MCTs are to be taken without access to books and materials.

3. *Observe the time limit*

Observe the overall time limit of $2\frac{1}{2}$ hours and try to spend no longer than an average of $2\frac{1}{2}$ minutes on each question. You will doubtless find that some of the questions can be answered in less time, whereas others require slightly more time – the questions vary in length and difficulty. However, the overall time limit reflects the standard of the MCT as a whole, and should not be exceeded.

4. *Read all four competing answers to each question before making a selection*

Whether a question is a problem-type question or a propositions-type question, you should *always* look at all four competing answers before making a selection. There are three good reasons for doing so.

First, an answer may refer to another answer or answers. For example, the question may set out a judge's ruling on a particular point of law, and conclude, 'Which of the following reasons could justify the judge's ruling?' [A] may then set out one reason and suggest that this *alone* could justify the ruling; [B] may set out a different reason and suggest that this *alone* could justify the ruling; and [C] may read, 'The reasons in both [A] and [B]'.

Secondly, even when you are relatively confident that you know the correct answer before you even look at the options on offer, and you are therefore tempted simply to select the 'correct' answer and to ignore the other answers, reading those other answers to check that they are indeed incorrect is the best way of confirming your initial selection.

Thirdly, there may well be occasions when you are unsure as to the correct answer. In these circumstances, it is often possible to identify the correct answer by the process of eliminating others which you know to be incorrect. Often you will find that the question-setter has included one answer which although somewhat plausible is clearly incorrect, and another which is also incorrect, although not quite so obviously, thereby reducing the effective choices from four to two – the two remaining answers will test whether you have understood the legal principle in question.

5. Deem the question-setter infallible

If your initial reaction, on reading a particular question and the four competing answers, is that you need more factual information before you can select the correct answer, or that there are two correct answers, or that the correct answer seems to have been omitted, quickly swallow your pride and re-read the question to see if there is something which you have missed or the importance of which you have failed to take note of on the first reading. If, having re-read the question and answers, you remain convinced that you need more information, or that there are two correct answers, or no correct answer, then select the answer which, in your opinion, gets nearest to being correct or is the best from which you have to make a choice.

6. Mark your performance

After you have completed each MCT – and probably after a break of suitable length – you will want to mark your performance. You will find the correct answers to MCT1 and MCT2 listed in Appendix 1 and Appendix 2 respectively. Award yourself one mark for each question that you have answered correctly. If you have selected one of the other three answers to the question, you should *not* subtract a mark – you simply gain no mark for that question. You may then rate your overall performance according to the following table.

Number of questions answered correctly in MCT1/MCT2	Comment
0–35	A performance ranging from the awful to the weak. At best, on 35, you are showing insufficient knowledge and comprehension in over 40% of all subjects tested.
36–44	A performance ranging from one of bare competence to competence. You are showing insufficient knowledge and comprehension in 26–40% of all subjects tested.
45–53	A performance ranging from the competent to the very competent. You are showing insufficient knowledge and comprehension in 11–25% of all subjects tested.
54–60	A performance ranging from the very competent to the outstanding. You are showing insufficient knowledge and comprehension in only 10% or less of all subjects tested.

7. Review your performance

After you have marked your performance, take a break! You need to be fully refreshed before you embark upon the most important part of the exercise, namely the review of your performance by reference to the written answers to the questions of MCT1 and MCT2, which you will find in Appendix 3 and Appendix 4, respectively. Thorough review is important because it allows you to identify with precision the gaps in your knowledge and understanding of the law with a view to further work or revision.

Look at *all* of the written answers, not just those to the questions which you got wrong. By looking at the answers to the questions which you answered correctly, you will usually confirm your understanding of the law. Sometimes, however, you may discover that although your answer was in fact correct, your reasoning was defective. Equally, you need to know the reasons for the answers at which you could only make an inspired guess.

MCT1

[TIME LIMIT: 2½ HOURS]

1. Sam and Sarah have been working together in partnership as hairdressers since 1990. They have considered incorporating their business but do not want to lose the benefits of operating as a partnership. Which of the following characteristics of their partnership business are *advantageous*?

(i)   Sam and Sarah as partners are jointly and severally liable for business debts.
(ii)   Sam and Sarah can keep the details of their partnership private.
(iii)   Sam and Sarah are both entitled to manage the business.
(iv)   As partners Sam and Sarah may pay a lower rate of income tax than they would as directors.

[A]   (i) and (iii).
[B]   (ii) and (iii).
[C]   (i), (ii) and (iii).
[D]   (i), (iii) and (iv).

2. For how much of the company's debts are shareholders in a company limited by shares liable when the company is wound up?

[A]   They are liable to the full extent of those debts.
[B]   Their liability is limited to the amount they have paid for their shares.
[C]   Their liability is limited to the fully paid up nominal value of their shareholding.
[D]   They are liable for an equal proportion of those debts shared equally between all the shareholders.

3. A company limited by shares is often the *preferred* business medium for which ONE of the following reasons?

[A] A company has perpetual succession.

[B] Shareholders have limited liability for the debts of the company.

[C] The requirement to disclose corporate matters to the Registrar of Companies.

[D] The ability of a company to hold property.

4. Which of the propositions set out below is INCORRECT?

[A] Many of the cases where the veil has been lifted involve situations where shareholders have been using the company for their own benefit or to avoid their obligations.

[B] It is not always easy to predict when the court will lift the veil of incorporation.

[C] The principle of the separate legal entity of companies remains strong.

[D] The courts will only lift the veil where there is fraud or illegality.

5. Which of the cases set out below DOES NOT support the following proposition?

'Each company in a group of companies . . . is a separate legal entity possessed of separate legal rights and liabilities.'

[A] *DHN Food Distributors Limited* v *Tower Hamlets London Borough Council* [1976] 1 WLR 852.

[B] *Woolfson and another* v *Strathclyde Regional Council* 1978 SLT 159.

[C] *Multinational Gas & Petroleum Co.* v *Multinational Gas & Petrochemical Services Ltd and others* [1983] Ch 258.

[D] *Adams* v *Cape Industries plc* [1990] Ch 433.

6. Jonah Lomas is the sole director and majority shareholder in Lomas Limited (his wife Mary is a nominee shareholder). Lomas Limited is a company which specialises in the manufacture of walking boots. Jonah has loaned £50,000 to the company secured by a debenture. The company's trading position appears to be weak and there is a risk of it going into liquidation. If the company does go into liquidation will Jonah be entitled to the return of his £50,000?

[A]   He will only be entitled to repayment when all the other creditors have been repaid.

[B]   This depends on whether the company has enough assets to pay all the creditors including Jonah.

[C]   The costs of liquidation will use up all the company's assets.

[D]   He will have priority for repayment over ordinary trade creditors but will only be repaid if the company has sufficient assets and there are no other secured creditors with a security which has priority to his debenture.

7. Which of the following is a correct statement about the effect of the contract under s. 14 of the Companies Act 1985?

[A]   A member may only enforce rights against the company.

[B]   The memorandum and articles are given contractual effect in respect of the member's rights as a director.

[C]   A member may enforce a personal right under that contract.

[D]   Only those members who have owned shares for a qualifying period of 2 years may enforce rights against the company.

8. Kenneth is a director of Brickmaker Limited. He has a power of veto set out in the company's articles over all decisions made by the board of directors concerning financial matters. Without consulting him the board has approved an increase in the salaries of all employees of the company. The company is now intending to ratify the board's decision at a general meeting to be held next week. How can Kenneth best enforce his power of veto?

[A] He should commence proceedings for an injunction restraining the company and the directors from acting on the resolution.

[B] He should bring an action for breach of the contract under s. 14 of the Companies Act 1985.

[C] This is not a matter over which his power of veto is operative.

[D] He should bring an action in his capacity as director of the company.

9. Dylan and Ewan were formerly directors of Camerahire Limited ('the company'). The other shareholders in the company, Beatrice and Candide, voted for the removal of Dylan and Ewan as directors under s. 303 of the Companies Act 1985. They believed that Dylan and Ewan had been incompetent as directors and had failed to consider the interests of the shareholders as a whole. Dylan and Ewan have 12% each of the shares in the company and wish to retain their shareholdings. Beatrice and Candide have proposed a special resolution at the next general meeting of the company that the articles be amended to include a provision that all former directors must transfer their shares to the other shareholders in the company within 6 months of their ceasing to be directors of the company. What is the correct advice to give to Dylan and Ewan?

[A] Beatrice and Candide must be able to show that the power of alteration of the articles is being exercised *bona fide* for the benefit of the company as a whole.

[B] The alteration is not valid if it applies to all members of the company.

[C] The alteration will have to be passed by a special resolution.

[D] Dylan and Ewan must be able to demonstrate that this change to the articles seriously affects their personal position within the company.

10. Aliyu, Bertrand, Cary and David are involved with Gromore Limited ('the company'). Aliyu is the finance director and owns 150 shares. Bertrand is the company's solicitor and owns 150 shares. Cary is the sales director and has no shares in the company. David is the managing director of the company and owns 200 shares. There is a provision in the articles of association which states that all disputes between directors will be referred to arbitration. David and Aliyu have disagreed over the dismissal of 2 key employees. How should the matter be resolved?

[A] Bertrand in his capacity as company solicitor should bring an action to enforce the provisions of the articles.

[B] The matter should be referred to arbitration and this could be enforced by any of the shareholders in the company.

[C] David as managing director should resolve the matter.

[D] Bertrand should refer the matter to arbitration and if the directors fail to comply he should then bring an injunction to enforce the provisions of the articles.

11. Jane and Isobel intend to set up a company. They have given instructions to their solicitors to form a company called 'J & I Designs Limited'. Before the company has actually been incorporated Jane decides to buy some office equipment which has been substantially reduced in a sale. She signs the contract with the supplier in the following way: 'Jane Brown for and on behalf of J & I Designs Limited'. Three days later the company is incorporated. What will be Jane's liability under the contract?

[A] She will have no liability for the items purchased.

[B] She should ensure that the contract is novated to the company on incorporation.

[C] She will be personally liable under the contract.

[D] The supplier will have to enforce the contract against J & I Designs Limited.

12. Which of the following propositions was illustrated by the decision in *Ashbury Railway Carriage & Iron Co. Ltd* v *Riche* (1857) LR 7 HL 653?

[A] A shareholder in a company is entitled to know for what purpose his money is being used.
[B] The company should not enter into contracts which are outside its legal capacity.
[C] The purpose of the memorandum of association is to protect the investor in the company.
[D] An *ultra vires* act could not be authorised or ratified by a unanimous decision of the shareholders.

13. What is the effect of s. 35 of the Companies Act 1985 as inserted by s. 108(1) of the Companies Act 1989?

[A] Members can prevent the company entering into transactions.
[B] A third party is always protected when it contracts with a limited company.
[C] Third parties are protected when they enter into a transaction with a company which has been approved by all the directors at a board meeting.
[D] Although acts done by a company cannot be invalidated due to incapacity under the memorandum members can still bring proceedings to restrain the directors from entering into an *ultra vires* transaction.

14. In 1995 Mortimer Limited ('Mortimer') borrowed £400,000 from Loanshires plc. The main objects clause of Mortimer is 'to act as a car dealer and a spare parts garage'. Mortimer has an additional objects clause which states that the directors may enter into any transaction which they believe to be in the best interests of the company. All 3 directors of Mortimer decide that Mortimer needs to expand into the area of rally car racing and purchase of rally cars. They will be using the loan from Loanshires plc for these purposes. Can Loanshires plc enforce the loan?

[A] The business of rally car racing and purchase of rally cars is *ultra vires* and therefore the loan is unenforceable.

[B] Provided that Loanshires plc acted in good faith in granting the loan and in dealing with Mortimer they can enforce the loan.

[C] The loan can be enforced because it was a decision made by the directors in the best interests of the company.

[D] The loan is enforceable provided that it was validly executed.

15. What would your answer to question 14 have been if the loan had been made in 1982?

[A] The business of rally car racing and purchase of rally cars is *ultra vires* and therefore the loan is unenforceable.

[B] Provided that Loanshires plc acted in good faith in granting the loan and in dealing with Mortimer they can enforce the loan.

[C] The loan can be enforced because it was a decision made by the directors in the best interests of the company.

[D] The loan is enforceable provided that it was validly executed.

16. Which of the following statements is INCORRECT?

[A] The shareholders of the company in general meeting may only interfere in the management of the company by special resolution.

[B] The only power reserved to the shareholders in general meeting to act by an ordinary resolution is to remove a director of the company.

[C] The shareholders in general meeting have a general power to interfere with the board's power by ordinary resolution.

[D] A company may adopt any form of articles to distribute the powers of management.

17. Norman has been offered the post of non-executive director of Berkleys Bank plc. He has been offered the post because of his wide range of contacts which he made in his previous job which was in public life. What ADVICE would you give to Norman to help him to ensure that he satisfies the standard of care he owes as a non-executive director?

[A] He should ensure that he is given sufficient information to enable him to make a proper contribution to the decisions made by the board of directors of the bank.

[B] Non-executive directors should bring a wide range of skills and expertise to the board.

[C] Non-executive directors are required and recommended by the Cadbury Report to be included on the board of every company.

[D] There are proposals for reform to introduce a two-tier board of directors.

18. Margaret is a 73% shareholder in Montague Services Limited ('the company'). The other 3 shareholders, Norma, Oliver and Pamela, are all directors of the company. All the directors have been accustomed to asking Margaret for advice about management of the company although she is not on the board. Margaret has suggested a scheme whereby the company pays £100,000 to her personally so that she can then invest the money in an Isle of Man trust account. She intends to repay the capital plus interest to the company in 3 years' time. Norma, Oliver and Pamela come to you for advice. What is the correct interpretation of this situation?

[A] Margaret will only have any liability as a shareholder of the company.

[B] Margaret is acting as a shadow director of the company and as such is as culpable in every respect as if she were a member of the board.

[C] The liability for any loss will be shared equally between all the shareholders.

[D] The directors are fully aware of the plan and may be acting in breach of their duties towards the shareholders but Margaret will not have any liability as she is not a director of the company.

19. Jack and Josephine are two of the directors of Waterflow Limited. The company has articles in the form of Table A unamended. The company has recently made a lot of profits by hiring water tankers to two large water companies in the North of England to transport water to alleviate problems caused by the lack of rain. Jack and Josephine have proposed at the board meeting that the directors award themselves a massive pay rise which would have the effect of taking the salary of the average director from £40,000 to £80,000. What advice would you give Jill, another director of the company, about what the directors need to do to ensure that this salary increase is permitted?

[A] The directors may award themselves whatever salary increase they wish.
[B] Excessive salary payments may prejudice the minority share-holders and creditors of the company therefore the directors may not increase their salaries.
[C] The directors need to disclose their service agreements to the shareholders of the company at the registered office of the company under s. 318 of the Companies Act 1985.
[D] Table A states that the directors' salaries need to be approved by the members in general meeting by an ordinary resolution.

20. Lorna and her two sisters Caroline and Polly have an equal shareholding in their company which deals with magazine publish-ing. They are also all directors of the company. They all wish to ensure that none of them can be removed by the shareholders from their position as directors of the company. Which of the following is the best way of protecting their positions as directors whilst they all three have equal shareholdings in the company?

[A] They should entrench the position of directors of the company by a provision in the articles which gives weighted voting rights to a director on any resolution to remove that person as a director of the company.
[B] They should draw up a shareholders' agreement.
[C] The only way to protect their position fully is to hold a majority of the voting rights on shares in the company.
[D] All three directors should be issued with long term service contracts.

21. Consider the following statements:

(i) The company is a separate entity from its shareholders.
(ii) The court refuses to be involved in disputes over how a company is operated.
(iii) The company can only operate effectively if majority rule prevails.
(iv) In order to bring a derivative action shareholders must show that there has been a fraud on the minority.

Which of the statements above are correct statements of the *rationale* behind the rule in *Foss* v *Harbottle* (1843) 2 Hare 461?

[A] i and iv.
[B] i and ii.
[C] ii, iii and iv.
[D] ii and iv.

22. Which of the following statements is NOT a correct statement of the grounds which must be established before a minority shareholder brings a derivative action under the fraud on the minority exception to the rule in *Foss* v *Harbottle* (1843) 2 Hare 461?

[A] That there has been a clear example of fraud as defined under the common law perpetrated against the company.
[B] That there has been a fraud on the minority shareholders in the company by those in control.
[C] That the majority are in control.
[D] That the majority will not permit an action to be brought in the name of the company.

23. Darrell, Elvis and Frances each hold one third of the shares in Sweet Limited. The company has been profitable in the last 3 years. Darrell and Elvis are the only two directors of the company and have not declared any dividends for the last 3 years and have refused to give Frances any explanation. What advice would you give Frances as to which of the following would be the most appropriate action to take if she wishes the company to remain in existence?

[A] She should bring a representative action against Darrell and Elvis for failure to declare dividends.

[B] She should bring a personal action for breach of the articles of association against Darrell and Elvis for their failure to declare dividends.

[C] She should immediately make an application for the company to be wound up under s. 122(1)(g) of the Insolvency Act 1986.

[D] She should bring a derivative action under the exception to the rule in *Foss* v *Harbottle* (1843) 2 Hare 461 if she can establish there has been a fraud on the minority.

24. Which of the following is NOT an example of a practical situation when the court will consider a petition under s. 459 of the Companies Act 1985?

[A] Where a rights issue is proposed which cannot be exercised by a majority shareholder.

[B] Failure to appoint a shareholder as a director of the company.

[C] The payment of low dividends to shareholders.

[D] Exclusion of the minority from the management of the company.

25. Which of the following orders is not available for the court to make when a petition for unfairly prejudicial conduct is successful?

[A] An order that the minority shareholder's shares are bought by the members of the company or by the company itself.

[B] Such order as the court thinks fit.

[C] An order that the minority shareholder's shares are valued as at the date of that shareholder becoming a member of the company.

[D] That the court may regulate the conduct of the company's affairs in the future.

26. You act for Cumbrae plc ('the company'). The company is listed on the London Stock Exchange and manufactures equipment for use on oil rigs. There has been a claim lodged against the company which if successful will be worth £240 million for the manufacture of faulty equipment. It is also feared that the claim will affect the company's share price and the reputation of the company. Hilary is a surveyor who does not work for the company but has been involved in investigating the faulty goods. She tells her friend Isobel about the potential claim and warns her to sell all her shares in the company as soon as she can. Isobel subsequently sells all her shares in the company. Greg is a waiter who works at the Golden Bay Hotel. He overheard the Managing Director of the company discussing the claim with his solicitor. Greg has now sold all his shares in the company at a loss but needed to sell his shares to pay off his overdraft. Consider the following statements:

(i)   Hilary is a primary insider.
(ii) Hilary has committed the offence of encouraging to deal.
(iii) Hilary is guilty of serious professional misconduct.
(iv) Hilary has committed the offence of disclosing information.

Which 2 offences have been committed by Hilary under the Criminal Justice Act 1993?

[A] i and ii.
[B] ii and iii.
[C] ii and iv.
[D] i and iii.

27. In question 26 what offence under the Criminal Justice Act 1993 has been committed by Isobel?

[A] She is a secondary insider and deals in securities.
[B] She is a primary insider.
[C] Disclosing information.
[D] Encouraging another to deal in securities.

28. In question 26 what offence under the Criminal Justice Act 1993 has been committed by Greg?

[A] Dealing in securities in possession of inside information as a primary insider.

[B] No offence has been committed – Greg has not received information from an inside source.

[C] Greg is a secondary insider but may have a defence if he could show that he would have sold the shares anyway to pay off his overdraft.

[D] Encouraging another to deal in securities.

29. Arran Limited is a company which owns caravan parks in South Wales. As part of a plan to diversify the ownership of Arran Limited the employees have been given the chance to purchase shares in the company. There is a possibility that the major site owned on the Gower peninsula will be developed next year by an outside developer. The effect of this will be substantially to increase the value of the company. Fiona the development manager has taken up her share allocation and has told two of the other employees that it would be 'worth their while' to take up the share offer but has refused to say any more. Consider the following statements:

(i) Fiona is in breach of the duty of confidentiality owed to her employer.

(ii) No offence has been committed by Fiona under the Criminal Justice Act 1993 (CJA) because the information she gave was not sufficiently detailed.

(iii) No offence has been committed under the CJA because the information is already in the public domain.

(iv) No offence has been committed under the CJA because Arran Limited is not a company listed on a regulated exchange.

Which of the above statements are correct?

[A] ii and iii.
[B] i and iv.
[C] ii and iv.
[D] i and ii.

30. Consider the following statements:

(i) The information is inside information.
(ii) The inside information relates to particular securities or a particular issue.
(iii) The individual has the information from an inside source and knows that it is from an inside source.
(iv) The individual has the requisite intention.

From the above statements, what is necessary to show that an individual has 'information as an insider' which is the central requirement of each of the three main offences under s. 57(1) of the Criminal Justice Act 1993?

[A] i, iii and iv.
[B] ii and iii.
[C] i and iii.
[D] ii, iii and iv.

31. Marjoram plc issues a fixed charge to Dill Bank plc on 1 June in return for a loan of £200,000. Marjoram plc issues a floating charge to Basil Limited on 12 June in respect of past and future indebtedness. On 21 June Marjoram plc goes into insolvent liquidation. What advice would you give to Basil Limited about the validity of its floating charge on the winding up of Majoram plc?

[A] The bank is a secured creditor.
[B] If the floating charge has been registered Basil Limited will rank below preferential creditors for the whole of the monies owed by Majoram plc.
[C] If the floating charge has been registered Basil Limited will rank below preferential creditors to the extent of any fresh consideration advanced to it on or after the granting of the floating charge.
[D] Charges need to be registered within 21 days of their creation.

32. What is the test applied to ascertain whether a director has carried out wrongful trading?

[A] The court looks at the conclusions which would be reached by a reasonable person.

[B] The test applied is both objective and subjective, looking at the steps which would be taken by a reasonably diligent person with the qualities which would be reasonably expected of a person in that position and with the qualities possessed by that particular person.

[C] The test applied to a director is that in *Re City Equitable Fire Insurance Co. Ltd* [1925] Ch 407.

[D] A director is penalised for not meeting the standards required under the Insolvency Act 1986.

33. Peace Whitehouse have been appointed as the liquidators on the liquidation of Caramel Limited. There is a fixed charge which has been granted to the bank and substantial sums of money are owed to the Inland Revenue and employees have not been paid for 3 months. Percy is an ordinary trade creditor of Caramel Limited. What advice would you give him about his chances of being paid the monies owed to him?

[A] The fixed charge will take priority as there is security for the debt owed.

[B] He should challenge the costs of the liquidators Peace Whitehouse if they seem to be excessive.

[C] As an unsecured creditor Percy will rank after the fixed charge, costs of the liquidation and monies owed to the Inland Revenue and the employees.

[D] The debts of all creditors in each class rank *pari passu.*

34. Consider the following statements:

(i) They are appointed by the court.
(ii) They are appointed by a creditor with a floating charge over the assets of the company.
(iii) Once they have been appointed no proceedings can be commenced to recover assets.
(iv) Once appointed they must act in the best interests of the creditor that appointed them in preference to the interests of all other creditors.

Which of the statements are correct statements about administrative receivers which does NOT apply to administrators?

[A] i and ii.
[B] i and iii.
[C] ii and iv.
[D] i, ii and iii.

35. Which of the statements below sets out some of the problems with the offence of wrongful trading under s. 214 of the Insolvency Act 1986?

[A] It imposes a civil offence and not criminal liability.
[B] There is no requirement to show intention to defraud creditors.
[C] It is difficult to ascertain the time at which the directors knew or ought to have concluded that there was no reasonable prospect of avoiding liquidation.
[D] Section 214 imposes a new objective standard on directors in the standard of competence expected of them.

36. Derek, Ken and Denis are the directors and equal shareholders of County Hall Limited ('CHL') a company which runs a hotel called County Hall in London. An opportunity has been proposed to Derek and Ken for an all-year-round booking of Japanese businessmen who are willing to pay high rates for their hotel accommodation. Derek and Ken have fallen out with Denis and decide to form another company to lease another city centre hotel and take this business which is worth £12m per annum. What action can Denis take?

[A] This may amount to unfairly prejudicial conduct and he could bring an action under s. 459 of the Companies Act 1985.

[B] CHL could sue Derek and Ken for the profit they have made under the contract which properly belonged to CHL.

[C] Any action Denis takes depends on whether the contract was offered to Derek and Ken because of their skill in the hotel trade as well as their position as directors of CHL.

[D] Denis cannot take any action unless the board of CHL had decided not to take up this contract.

37. Matthew Jones is the financial director of Galilee Ltd a fish products company. His wife Mary is a computer programmer and sole director of Highline Ltd. Three companies have tendered for work at Galilee Ltd including Highline Ltd. Matthew was on the panel of directors that decided which computer company Galilee Ltd would appoint. What action should Matthew take at the board meeting at which the contract between Galilee Ltd and Highline Ltd is approved?

[A] He will be unable to vote by virtue of Articles 94 and 95 of Table A.

[B] He should declare his interest in the contract under s. 317 of the Companies Act 1985.

[C] He must resign from his position as director of the company if he votes in favour of Highline Ltd being awarded the contract.

[D] He need take no action provided that he acts *bona fide* in the best interests of the company.

38. Martha and Mary are the directors of Bodycare Limited ('the company') which manufactures expensive ointments and perfumes. Mary has little business experience but is an excellent chemist. She is invaluable to the company but refuses to learn anything about the finances of the company or even to attend a course on basic accounts. Martha is an accountant and is very financially astute and well aware of her duties as financial director. The company is in financial difficulties but continues to trade. Mary seems unaware of these financial difficulties. The company has operated for 10 years during which time both Mary and Martha have been directors. What risk do Mary and Martha run if the company goes in to liquidation?

[A] Both Martha and Mary will have to contribute to the assets of the company despite Mary's unbusinesslike attitude.

[B] Martha may have to contribute to the assets of the company. As financial director she should have been aware of the company's financial position.

[C] Mary will not be liable to contribute to the assets of the company as she has never been involved in the financial aspects of the business.

[D] Martha may face criminal liability due to her failure to use her financial expertise.

39. Candide is the sole director of Competitive Marketing Limited ('CML') a small marketing agency. The shares in the company are owned by Comparative plc. At a recent board meeting of CML Candide awarded herself a termination payment of £100,000 which she believes is due to her under her service contract. What will be the effect of Candide failing to declare her interest in the payment of £100,000?

[A] The payment of £100,000 will be voidable for lack of disclosure regardless of anything in the company articles.

[B] As sole director Candide is not under any requirement to disclose her interest to herself.

[C] Unless Candide got the approval of Comparative plc to the termination payment it will be invalid in any event.

[D] The payment of £100,000 will be valid at common law depending on the articles although failure to comply with s. 317 of the Companies Act 1985 will mean that Candide is liable to a fine.

40. Paul and Michelle are the only directors of Tree Limited and Paul is the managing director. He and Michelle resolve to issue 100 shares to Alan their friend on 1 January even though the company does not require more capital because they wish to offer him a job as an accountant and shares in the company. Six months later they enter into a contract with Alan for the purchase of a car worth £5,000. After the car has been bought by the company they then sell it to Michelle for £1,000. They do not inform any of the other shareholders of this transaction. Which of the following statements are correct?

(i) The issue of shares to Alan was an issue for a purpose other than to raise capital.
(ii) The sale of the car to Michelle was a substantial property transaction which was not properly approved.
(iii) The contract for the sale of the car may be voidable at the option of the company.
(iv) Paul and Michelle may be liable to compensate the company for any loss suffered.

[A] i and iv.
[B] i, ii, iii and iv.
[C] iii and iv.
[D] i and ii.

41. Which of the following statements accords with the definition of a shadow director in s. 741 of the Companies Act 1985?

[A] An individual who has never been appointed as a director but holds himself out as a director to third parties and acts as a director.
[B] A person who may or may not have been appointed as a director but in accordance with whose directions or instructions the directors of a company were accustomed to act.
[C] An individual who has been validly appointed as a director of a company.
[D] A professional adviser to a board of directors.

42. ABC plc is a holding company of 25 subsidiary companies within its group of companies. One of these subsidiary companies XYZ Limited manufactures dangerous chemicals. Following a serious accident at the factory XYZ Limited has been threatened with massive claims for compensation by the employees of the company. If these claims are successful XYZ Limited will go into liquidation. What will be the *liability of ABC plc* for these claims if XYZ Limited cannot afford to pay?

[A] ABC plc will be liable for the debts of its subsidiaries as the group will always be treated as a single economic entity.

[B] XYZ Limited is a separate legal entity and as such liable for its own debts.

[C] The creditors of XYZ Limited should bring an action against ABC plc to recover any debts owing to them which are unsatisfied by XYZ Limited.

[D] ABC plc will usually have no liability for the debts of XYZ Limited.

43. What is the essential difference between the treatment of groups of companies for tax and accounting purposes and the way that they are treated for most other legal purposes?

[A] The way in which a group of companies is treated for tax and accounting purposes and for all other purposes is to look at the economic reality of the situation.

[B] The courts generally treat a group of companies as a single economic entity for all purposes.

[C] For the purposes of tax and accounting a group of companies is treated as a single economic entity but for all other purposes the companies in a group are treated separately.

[D] The courts will only lift the veil of incorporation to apply a taxation statute.

44. The articles of association of Main Limited, a paper manufacturing company state that any decision by the board to enter into a contract for supply of materials must be authorised in advance by the members of the company in general meeting. All the directors at a recent board meeting authorised a contract between the company and Timber Limited for the supply of materials without obtaining the consent of the members in general meeting. Consider the following statements:

(i) Timber Limited can rely on the rule in *Royal British Bank* v *Turquand* (1856) 6 E & B 327 that all internal procedures have been followed correctly.
(ii) Timber Limited can rely on s. 35A of the Companies Act 1985 if they are a party dealing with the company in good faith.
(iii) Until the contract is ratified Timber Limited cannot be sure that the contract will be binding.
(iv) Whether the contract is binding depends on whether Timber Limited believed the directors had authority to enter into the contract.

Which of the above statements apply to whether the contract between Main Limited and Timber Limited is binding?

[A] i and ii.
[B] ii and iv.
[C] i and iv.
[D] iii and iv.

45. Marilyn is the assistant to one of the directors of Misfits Limited a ticket agency company. Yesterday she signed a contract for the purchase of tickets to the ballet at Sadlers Wells Theatre. These tickets cost in total £400,000. Previously Marilyn had ordered tickets up to a value of £2,000 from Sadlers Wells. She had no authority to buy the tickets. Is Misfits Limited bound by the contract with Sadlers Wells?

[A] Marilyn had no actual authority to enter into the contract and therefore Misfits Limited will not be bound by the contract.

[B] Although Marilyn had no actual authority to enter into the contract she may have apparent authority for the transaction and Misfits Limited will be bound by the contract. Misfits Limited may be able to claim against Marilyn personally.

[C] Marilyn will be personally liable for the contract.

[D] By virtue of her position in the company Marilyn clearly would have authority for this kind of transaction.

46. The directors of Brown plc have been threatened by a takeover by Blue plc. In order to try and prevent the takeover happening the directors of Brown plc allotted sufficient of the unissued share capital to a trust fund for the benefit of the employees. The directors were of the opinion that the takeover was not in the best interests of the company. On what grounds can this allotment of shares be challenged by a shareholder?

[A] The power to issue shares should only be exercised by the directors acting in good faith which is not the case here.

[B] Shares issued improperly are not valid and do not carry any voting rights.

[C] The directors were not acting in the best interests of the employee trust fund.

[D] The fiduciary power of the directors to issue shares had been exercised for an improper purpose.

47. John is a partner in JB Furniture Supplies and also a director of Manifold Enterprises Limited (Manifold). Manifold agreed to purchase a new table and chairs for the board room from JB Furniture Supplies. Manifold has not paid the money owed to the partnership for the chairs. John made no declaration to Manifold as to his conflict of interest. What advice would you give the partnership as to whether it can recover the money from Manifold owed for the furniture?

[A] The partnership can clearly establish that the money is owed to it by Manifold.

[B] John should have declared his interest in the partnership before purchasing the table and chairs – as he failed to do so the partnership will be unable to claim the money from Manifold.

[C] Manifold can argue that the contract is voidable because John had a conflict of interest which he failed to declare.

[D] The company should sue John personally for the cost of the table and chairs.

48. Mary is a director of Lancome Limited which has net assets of £100,000. She contracts with the company to buy a car from the company for her own use. The price paid for the car is £15,000 which is considerably less than the market value of the car. Mary declared her interest in the contract at the board meeting at which the purchase of the car was discussed. What is the effect of the transaction?

[A] It is an approved contract as Mary declared her interest to the board of directors.

[B] The contract is illegal and voidable as it has not been approved by the company in general meeting and it is a substantial property transaction.

[C] The contract is automatically void as it is not in the best interests of the company.

[D] Mary is likely to be removed from the board of directors.

49. The directors of Gannet Limited propose to award themselves service contracts for 9 years commencing on 1 January. What advice would you give the directors about the effect of these service contracts?

[A] Where service contracts contain a term for more than 5 years then that term is void unless it is first approved by the company in general meeting.

[B] Due to the excessive length of the term the company may be able to terminate the contract on reasonable notice if there has been gross misconduct.

[C] The contracts will be valid provided that they have been approved by the directors.

[D] The directors will be able to rely on all the terms of the service contracts.

50. Mandy, Lara and Leo own 33% each of the shares in Richlife Limited and are also each directors of the company. Mandy and Lara want to dismiss Leo as a director. The company has articles in the form of Table A unamended. What advice would you give to Leo as to whether he can be removed?

[A] Under s. 303 of the Companies Act 1985 an ordinary resolution is required to remove a director. Mandy and Lara can therefore remove Leo as they own 66% of the shares in the company between them.

[B] Leo will have the protection of compensation under his service contract.

[C] Mandy and Lara will be unable to remove Leo because he has the benefit of weighted voting rights.

[D] Leo should have built in protection for himself in the articles to prevent his removal.

51. Falconer Limited ('Falconer') is a private company limited by shares with articles in the form of Table A. It is proposed to sell the shares in Falconer to Magna Limited ('Magna') for £5m. Magna cannot raise all the money required for this share purchase and proposes to use the assets of Falconer to secure a bank loan from Megabank plc for £3m. Which of the following statements is true with respect to the use of the assets of Falconer to give this security?

[A] This is clearly financial assistance by Falconer and as such will be prohibited and illegal.
[B] This financial assistance can only be given if strict statutory procedures are followed which then make the financial assistance permissible.
[C] The Companies Acts make provisions to ensure maintenance of share capital.
[D] Financial assistance is only permitted if it falls within one of the specific exceptions to the prohibition as set out in s. 153, CA 1985.

52. Consider the following statements:

(i)   A parent company A plc guaranteeing a loan for a third party B plc to purchase shares in A plc's subsidiary company C plc.
(ii) A company D Limited allowing its assets to be used to secure a loan for the purchase of its assets by E Limited.
(iii) The declaration of a lawful dividend by a public company F plc.
(iv) A gift by H plc to enable J plc to purchase the shares in H plc.

Which of the above transactions are financial assistance which would be PROHIBITED?

[A] i and ii.
[B] iii and iv.
[C] i, ii and iii.
[D] i and iv.

53. Munificent Limited has made a loss in the financial year 1995–96 of £3,000. In the previous 2 years its profit was:

1994–95 £6,000.
1993–94 £2,000.

Which of the following is a correct statement as to whether it is possible for the directors of Munificent Limited to declare a dividend at the end of 1996 although the company has made a loss in that year?

[A] This decision will be made solely at the discretion of the directors regardless of all other factors.

[B] Dividends are treated as a distribution of profit if the company has not made a profit it cannot declare a dividend.

[C] In order to declare a dividend a company must have sufficient distributable profits available when all realised losses have been deducted from realised profits. The directors could therefore declare a dividend.

[D] This will depend on whether the profits arise from income or capital.

54. Fiona, Frederica and Ferdinand are the only directors and shareholders of Sandico Limited ('the company') which has articles in the form of Table A unamended. Fiona wants to leave the company and has suggested that the company could purchase the shares which she owns in the company. Such a purchase would have to be out of capital. In what circumstances could the company purchase Fiona's shares *out of capital*?

[A] The company cannot purchase her shares because it is not a company listed on the Stock Exchange.

[B] Purchase of shares is only permissible out of profits or out of the proceeds of a fresh issue of shares.

[C] The company can only purchase its own shares if it is authorised to do so by the articles.

[D] The company can purchase Fiona's shares out of capital provided that this is authorised by a special resolution and the directors make a declaration that the company will be able to pay its debts for the next 12 months.

55. Consider the following statements:

(i) A company may not purchase its own shares.
(ii) A company may not give financial assistance for the purchase of its own shares.
(iii) A company may issue different classes of shares such as ordinary or preference shares with different rights attaching to them.
(iv) Directors may only issue shares if they have authority to do so.
(v) Dividends must only be paid out of profits.

Which of the above statements are examples of the doctrine of maintenance of capital?

[A] i and ii.
[B] i, ii and v.
[C] i, ii and iv.
[D] ii, iii and iv.

56. Which of the following is the main *disadvantage* of a successful application for the winding up of a company under s. 122(1)(g) of the Insolvency Act 1986 on the grounds that it is just and equitable to do so?

[A] It is a drastic remedy in that the company ceases to exist.
[B] It is generally only available for a quasi partnership company.
[C] It provides a remedy where there has been a breach of equitable rights and a breakdown in mutual trust and agreement.
[D] It should only be included as an alternative to an order under s. 459 of the Companies Act 1985 as a remedy if it is the only relief to which the petitioner is entitled or it is the relief that the petitioner may prefer.

57. Ned is the financial director of Magicarpet Limited ('the company'), a carpet retailer. Since 1 January he has been aware that the company has been in financial difficulties but he hoped that things would improve. On 1 February he arranged for the purchase of large quantities of carpet. On 1 April the company's major customer went into liquidation. On 1 June the company went into liquidation. The other directors were surprised about the liquidation because Ned had kept financial information to himself so the other directors did not worry. What liability may Ned and his fellow directors have incurred?

[A] Ned is clearly guilty of fraudulent and wrongful trading.

[B] Ned alone is guilty of fraudulent trading.

[C] Ned alone is guilty of wrongful trading from at least 1 April onwards.

[D] Ned and all the other directors are likely to be guilty of wrongful trading.

58. Manic Limited has been compulsorily wound up by one of its creditors. The liquidator has discovered that the following creditors are due to be paid after the fixed charge has been cleared:

Inland Revenue PAYE £4,000
Customs and Excise VAT £2,200
Floating charge to Noble Investors Limited £4,800
Total costs of liquidation estimated at £9,000
Trade creditors £60,000

The total assets available for distribution are £40,000. What advice would you give Tom, a trade creditor, who is owed £3,000 about the amount of his debt he can expect to obtain from the liquidation?

[A] As an unsecured creditor Tom will not receive any payment on the liquidation of Manic Limited.

[B] Tom will receive two-thirds of the debt owed to him as will all other creditors in the same class.

[C] Tom will receive £1,000.

[D] Tom will be paid in full the £3,000 owed to him.

59. Megaflow plc ('the company') has made an offer to purchase all the shares in Bird plc ('Bird'). Both companies are listed on the Stock Exchange. Consider the following statements:

(i)   The directors must consider their own personal positions and prospects of being retained as directors after the takeover.
(ii) The directors must consider the prospects for Bird after the takeover and the likely effect on the value of shares in the future.
(iii) The directors must consider the price being offered for the shares.
(iv) The directors must consider interests of the shareholders and employees of Bird.

What factors must the directors of Bird plc take into account when they are deciding whether or not to recommend the offer to the shareholders?

[A]   i and ii.
[B]   ii, iii and iv.
[C]   i and ii.
[D]   i, ii and iii.

60. Hanover plc ('Hanover') is a company listed on the Stock Exchange. Some of the institutional investors have called a meeting to investigate whether the provisions of the Cadbury Code are being complied with. Hanover has a board of directors comprising Anna who is both chairman and chief executive, Bert the financial adviser and Kate the sales director. There are no other directors. Consider the following recommendations:

(i)   The chairman and chief executive should be different people. Hanover should consider appointing a new chairman.
(ii)   The financial director should form a remuneration committee which will comprise himself and two representatives of the shareholders.
(iii) The board of directors should meet less regularly and leave the control and management of the company to the chief executive.
(iv)   The company should appoint non-executive directors. Some of these non-executive directors will form the remuneration committee.

Which of the above would you do to ensure that the company complies with the Cadbury Code?

[A]   i, iii and iv.
[B]   i and ii.
[C]   ii and iii.
[D]   i and iv.

MCT2

[TIME LIMIT: 2½ HOURS]

1. Y plc decides to accept non-cash consideration as payment for its shares. In which of the following circumstances must Y plc obtain an independent valuation of the consideration in question?

[A] The allotment of redeemable preference shares.
[B] The allotment of bonus shares.
[C] The allotment of shares to the shareholders of another company in exchange for the transfer or cancellation of shares in that other company.
[D] The allotment of shares to the shareholders of another company in exchange for the acquisition of the assets and liabilities of that other company.

2. Which one of the following propositions is NOT an advantage of incorporation?

[A] A company has perpetual succession.
[B] Shareholders have limited liability for the debts of the company.
[C] The formalities required in ensuring the compliance with statutory requirements in respect of disclosure to the Registrar of Companies.
[D] The need to find and appoint independent directors.

3. An elective resolution which is available to a private limited company is an order to do which of the following?

[A] To change the name of the company.
[B] To increase the remuneration of its shareholders.
[C] To declare a distribution and dividend to its shareholders.
[D] To dispense with the laying of accounts and reports before a general meeting.

4. In breach of s. 80 of the Companies Act 1985 Julian, a director of Finance plc, issues and allots shares to Beryl. Which of the following propositions accurately reflects the position of both Julian and Beryl?

[A] Julian is in breach of his duties as a director and must compensate both Beryl and the company for any loss suffered.
[B] Beryl must return the shares to the company and Julian is liable to a fine.
[C] Julian will be liable to a fine, but Beryl will keep the shares and remain a member of the company.
[D] Julian is liable to a fine and will be obliged to pay compensation to Beryl.

5. Which of the following propositions is correct?

[A] The veil of incorporation prevents the courts from recognising groups of companies as one entity.
[B] The veil of incorporation will always be lifted by the court in order to recognise groups of companies.
[C] The courts will only lift the veil of incorporation to recognise groups of companies if legislation states that the group must be recognised.
[D] The courts are prepared to lift the veil and recognise groups of companies but only in limited and uncertain circumstances.

6. Joint plc has 2 directors, Tom and Beryl. In January, Beryl resigns from her position as director. Tom continues as the sole director of Joint plc and arranges for Joint plc to enter into a variety of trading contracts and credit agreements. Tom is now wondering whether he should continue as sole director or seek a replacement for Beryl. What is the correct advice to give to Tom?

[A] Every public and private company must have a minimum of 2 directors.

[B] Every public company must have 2 directors and every private company 1 director only.

[C] Every company can choose a minimum number of directors and that Tom should seek the amendment of the company's articles to permit the appointment of 1 director only.

[D] Tom should secure the passing of a special resolution authorising the appointment of 1 director only.

7. Using the facts of question 6 above, what advice would you give to Tom assuming that Tom and Beryl had been the only shareholders in Joint plc, and that Beryl has since ceased to be a shareholder and a director?

[A] A public company need have 1 shareholder only.

[B] All private and public companies must have a minimum of 2 shareholders.

[C] A public company must have a minimum of 2 shareholders.

[D] All public companies and private companies must have a minimum of 7 shareholders.

8. In which of the following ways and subject to what limitations may the shareholders of a company alter its article of association?

[A] By special resolution and in a manner which is *bona fide* in the interests of the company as a whole, that the alteration does not conflict with the memorandum of association or any statutory provisions.

[B] By ordinary resolution and in a manner which is *bona fide* in the interests of the company as a whole, and the alteration does not conflict with the memorandum of association.

[C] By special resolution for any reason whatsoever provided the alteration does not conflict with provisions in the memorandum of association.

[D] By ordinary resolution provided that the alteration is sanctioned by the court and does not conflict with provisions in the memorandum of association.

9. Robert is a director and shareholder of Railstation Limited. Railstation Limited's articles of association provide that all disputes between members and the company must initially be referred to arbitration. Robert is now in dispute with the company following the failure of Railstation Limited to honour an agreement to redeem part of Robert's shareholding. Which one of the following cases is relevant to Robert's claim against Railstation Limited?

[A] *Adams* v *Cape Industries plc* [1990] Ch 433.

[B] *Percival* v *Wright* [1902] 2 Ch 421.

[C] *Hickman* v *Kent or Romney Marsh Sheep-breeders' Association* [1915] 1 Ch 881.

[D] *Re Lee Behrens & Co. Ltd* [1932] 2 Ch 46.

10. Bert has been appointed as a director of Supaclass Limited under the articles of association which provide that his appointment is for a fixed period of 3 years. After only 1 year in appointment Supaclass Limited seek to remove Bert and alter the articles of association. Which one of the following cases is relevant to Bert's position?

[A] *Daniels* v *Daniels* [1978] Ch 406.
[B] *Southern Foundries (1926) Ltd* v *Shirlaw* [1940] AC 701.
[C] *Woolfson and another* v *Strathclyde Regional Council* 1978 SC (HL) 90.
[D] *Freeman & Lockyer* v *Buckhurst Park Properties (Mangal) Ltd and another* [1964] 2 QB 480.

11. Which one of the following accurately reflects the position of a promoter?

[A] Promoters are automatically entitled to remuneration from the company for the services they provide.
[B] Promoters are only entitled to remuneration from the company if the articles of association provide for remuneration.
[C] Promoters are automatically entitled to the preliminary expenses connected with the formation of a company, such as registration fees only.
[D] Promoters can only claim remuneration from a company if they can establish the existence of a binding contract with the company.

12. Elizabeth is the promoter of the company Zeal plc. Elizabeth decides that she would like to sell to Zeal plc some business premises owned by Elizabeth. The sale will result in Elizabeth enjoying a huge profit. Which one of the following propositions represents the best advice to Elizabeth, assuming she wishes to keep the profit on the sale of the business premises?

[A] Disclosure and approval of the sale and profit must be made to the first directors of the company who are all nominees of Elizabeth.

[B] Disclosure and approval of the sale must be made to all subscribers to the memorandum of association.

[C] No disclosure is required.

[D] Disclosure and approval must be to the subscribers to the memorandum and disclosure must be made in all material published to prospective shareholders inviting them to take up shares in the company.

13. Which of the following propositions *accurately* reflects s. 36C of the Companies Act 1985?

[A] The decision in *Newborne* v *Sensolid (Great Britain) Ltd* [1954] 1 QB 45 is confirmed, and promoters will not be liable on pre-incorporated contracts provided they sign 'as agent'.

[B] Promoters are liable on all pre-incorporation contracts provided they sign 'on behalf of' the company.

[C] Promoters are liable on all pre-incorporation contracts irrespective of whether they sign 'on behalf of' or as the company.

[D] It is the company not the promoter who will be liable on all pre-incorporation contracts.

14. Section 3A of the Companies Act 1985 provides that a company can do which of the following?

[A] Change its name at any time.
[B] Change its objects at any time.
[C] Enjoy the implied powers to do all things that it wishes.
[D] Carry on any trade or business whatsoever and enjoy all incidental powers.

15. Which of the following propositions was illustrated by the decision in *Re Introductions Ltd* [1970] Ch 199?

[A] A company cannot convert a power into an object through the use of an independent objects clause.
[B] All powers will stand as independent objects provided a clause to that effect is included in the company's memorandum of association.
[C] A company cannot convert an object into a power through the use of an independent objects clause.
[D] All powers and objects are free standing and independent.

16. Which of the following statements is correct?

[A] Members of a company no longer enjoy the right to prevent or object to an *ultra vires* act.
[B] Members of a company can still seek an injunction to prevent a company from acting *ultra vires*.
[C] It is only the directors of a company who can prevent a company from acting *ultra vires*.
[D] A company cannot in any circumstances act *ultra vires*.

17. Which of the following statements is correct?

[A] All *ultra vires* contracts remain unenforceable against the company.

[B] *Ultra vires* contracts can be enforced against their directors causing the company to act *ultra vires* only.

[C] Directors causing a company to act *ultra vires* can receive relief from their liability by an ordinary resolution of members.

[D] Members of a company can pass a special resolution relieving directors from liability for breach of duties in causing a company to act *ultra vires*.

18. The board of directors of Soames plc exceeds its authority and causes Soames plc to enter into an unauthorised contract with Lost Limited. Which of the following propositions accurately reflects the position of Lost Limited?

[A] The unauthorised contract can never be enforced.

[B] The unauthorised contract can only be enforced if Soames plc agrees to this.

[C] The unauthorised contract can be enforced provided Lost Limited acted in good faith.

[D] The unauthorised contract can be enforced even if Lost Limited acted in bad faith.

19. Which one of the following contracts remains voidable at the option of the company?

[A] An *ultra vires* contract.

[B] An unauthorised contract entered into in good faith with a director of the company.

[C] An unauthorised contract entered into in good faith with unconnected outsiders.

[D] An *ultra vires* contract made in bad faith.

20. Which of the following propositions was illustrated by the decision in *Royal British Bank* v *Turquand* (1856) 6 E & B 327?

[A] When dealing with a company, outsiders must check to ensure that all internal procedures have been complied with.
[B] Outsiders can ignore all internal procedures and requirements of a company, even when they possess knowledge that the internal procedures have not been complied with.
[C] Those persons dealing with a company are entitled to assume that the internal procedures of a company have been complied with in the absence of actual notice to the contrary.
[D] Those persons dealing with a company must ensure that all contracts are authorised by 2 directors of the company.

21. Which one of the following cases does NOT deal with the issue of the 'directing mind' of a company?

[A] *Tett* v *Phoenix Property & Investment Co. Ltd and Others* [1986] BCLC 149.
[B] *Tesco Supermarkets Ltd* v *Nattrass* [1972] AC 153.
[C] *El Ajou* v *Dollar Land Holdings plc* [1994] BCLC 464.
[D] *Re Supply of Ready Mixed Concrete (No. 2)* [1995] IAC 456.

22. Generally a company may be regarded as a entity to which criminal liability may attach, subject to a number of exceptions. Which one of the following is INCORRECT?

[A] A company cannot be convicted of a crime where the criminal act involves the commission of a physical act.
[B] A company may not be convicted of an offence where the punishment for the crime charged is a sentence incapable of being imposed on a company.
[C] A company cannot be charged with an offence which involves the driving of a vehicle.
[D] A company cannot be convicted of the offence of conspiracy.

23. Which of following statements is INCORRECT?

[A]   A company may be liable for torts of strict liability.
[B]   A company may be vicariously liable for the torts of its servants.
[C]   A company cannot be liable for a tort which involves proof of malice.
[D]   A company may be liable for a tort which involves proof of malice.

24. Julian has always held shares in Paper plc and registered his shareholding in the name of a nominee. Julian has recently acquired some more shares in Paper plc and he now owns 7% of voting shares in Paper plc. Which of the following represents the correct advice to be given to Julian?

[A]   Because he owns more than 5% of voting shares in Paper plc, he must notify the company and no longer hide behind the nominee.
[B]   Because he owns more than 3% of voting shares he must notify the company.
[C]   Julian need not notify the company of his purchase and interests.
[D]   The nominee must inform the company of Julian's interests.

25. Which of the following statements is INCORRECT?

[A]   Every company must keep a register of its members giving details of the extent of each member's shareholding in the company.
[B]   An incorrect entry on the register of members can be challenged for any purpose.
[C]   In order to challenge an entry on the register of members, a legitimate interest must be established.
[D]   Subscribers to a company's memorandum are deemed to have agreed to become members of the company.

26. The directors of Beckett Limited have refused to register a transfer of shares from Mike to Vicky. Which of the following represents the correct advice to Vicky?

[A] The directors of a company have no rights in any circumstances to refuse to register a share transfer.
[B] If power is given to the directors to refuse to register a share transfer the directors need not provide any reasons to explain their refusal.
[C] When directors refuse to register a transfer they must give reasons for the refusal within 2 months following the share transfer.
[D] The directors can only refuse to register a transfer of partly paid shares.

27. Which of the following class of shares are NOT subject to the general pre-emption rights contained in s. 89 of the Companies Act 1985?

[A] Ordinary shares.
[B] Preference shares.
[C] Employee shares
[D] Equity shares.

28. Blackwood plc issued a prospectus in accordance with the industry regulations. Unfortunately the prospectus provides some incorrect and misleading information. Which one of the following CANNOT be a defence available to Blackwood plc or its officers?

[A] That the subscriber was aware that the statement was untrue.
[B] That the company and its officers reasonably believed the statement to be true and accurate and had made reasonable enquiries to establish this.
[C] That the company and its officers reasonably believed the statement to be true and accurate up to the time of issuing that statement only.
[D] That the statement was accurate and fairly produced from an official public document.

29. Which of the following cases supports the proposition that:

'A company is entitled to include a weighted voting clause in its articles of association. Such a clause is accepted because it deals with a company's voting rights and a company is entitled to issue a share with special rights or restrictions.'

[A]   *Bushell* v *Faith* [1970] 1 All ER 53.
[B]   *Southern Foundries (1926) Ltd* v *Shirlaw* [1940] AC 701.
[C]   *Re Sevenoaks Stationers (Retail) Ltd* [1991] Ch 164.
[D]   *Peso Silver Mines Ltd (NPL)* v *Cropper* (1966) 58 DLR (2d) 1.

30. Which of the propositions set out below is correct?

[A]   All companies must have a minimum of 2 directors.
[B]   All private limited companies only must have a minimum of 2 directors.
[C]   All public limited companies must have a minimum of 2 directors.
[D]   The minimum number of directors in a public company must be stated in the articles of association and that number must be greater than 5 directors.

31. The articles of Super Supplies plc provide that each director must hold a minimum of 500 fully paid ordinary shares. Tom is a director of Super Supplies plc but only holds 200 fully paid ordinary shares. What advice would you give to Tom?

[A]   Where the articles prescribe a share qualification, the directors must acquire those shares within the specified time otherwise they must vacate their office.
[B]   No company is allowed to specify a minimum shareholding requirement for its directors.
[C]   Where a minimum shareholding requirement is specified, directors must be given a reasonable time of at least 6 months to acquire these shares.
[D]   All directors in public limited companies must hold a minimum of 1% of the companies' issued ordinary shares.

32. Which of the following propositions is INCORRECT?

[A] Directors are not entitled as of right to any remuneration.
[B] The articles of association may provide for the payment of directors' fees.
[C] All directors are appointed under service contracts entitling the director to a salary.
[D] If a director performs services which are not comprehended by the terms of any service contract, he may claim in *quantum meruit*.

33. Which case established the principle that, 'if directors are unable or unwilling to exercise the powers conferred upon them, whether by reason of there being no independent quorum or by reason of disputes among the directors, the company in general meeting can then perform the duties which the directors had to carry out'?

[A] *Barron* v *Potter* [1914] 1 Ch 895.
[B] *Salmon* v *Quin & Axtens Ltd* [1909] 1 Ch 311.
[C] *John Shaw & Sons (Salford) Ltd* v *Shaw and Shaw* [1935] 2 KB 113.
[D] *Pender* v *Lushington* (1877) 6 ChD 70.

34. Which of the following propositions is INCORRECT?

[A] The board can only delegate powers of management to a managing director if expressly empowered by the articles or by a resolution of the company.
[B] It is a statutory requirement that all companies must nominate and appoint a member of its board to act as managing director of the company.
[C] A managing director can be dismissed from his directorship at any stage by an ordinary resolution of the members of the company.
[D] If the board of directors acquiesce in one of their number acting as a managing director then he will have the ostensible authority of a managing director.

35. David is appointed as the company secretary for Mode plc. David promptly orders some computer disks in the name of Mode plc but he uses these disks for his own private purposes and keeps the disks at his home address. Mode plc discovers this and refuse to pay the invoice received for the disks. Which one of the following propositions accurately reflects the position of Mode plc?

[A] A company secretary does not enjoy any rights to order goods on behalf of a company and therefore the contract for the computer disks is void.

[B] A company secretary can only bind the company on contracts expressly authorised by the board of directors.

[C] A company secretary can only bind the company on contracts for goods when those goods are used by the company for business purposes.

[D] A company secretary enjoys the general powers of an agent irrespective of whether goods ordered are actually used for the business purposes of the company.

36. Which one of the following statements is correct?

[A] A contract of employment with a director for a period exceeding 5 years and containing a term under which the company cannot terminate the employment by notice, or can do so only in specified circumstances, is void unless it is first approved by a resolution of the company in general meeting.

[B] If a contract of employment with a director for a period exceeding 5 years contains a term under which the company cannot terminate the employment by notice, or can do so only in specified circumstances, then that term only is void unless it is first approved by a resolution of the company in general meeting.

[C] All contracts of employment and terms of employment with a director must first be approved by resolution of the company in general meeting.

[D] A special resolution is required before contracts of employment can be issued to directors of a company.

37. Which one of the following is UNLIKELY to be a ground for the disqualification of a director?

[A] An act of commercial misjudgement.
[B] A conviction of an indictable offence in respect of the management of a company's property.
[C] A persistent default in respect of the filing of an annual report with the Register of Companies.
[D] A finding of fraudulent trading under s. 213 of the Insolvency Act 1986.

38. Sandra is a director of Joy plc and is responsible for negotiating sales contracts. An established client of Joy plc indicates that it wishes to contract with Sandra in her personal capacity only. The same client explains that it will not contract with Joy plc now or in the future. Which one of the following cases applies to Sandra's situation?

[A] *Pender* v *Lushington* (1877) 6 ChD 70.
[B] *Greenhalgh* v *Arderne Cinemas Ltd* [1951] Ch 286.
[C] *Barron* v *Potter* [1914] 1 Ch 895.
[D] *Industrial Development Consultants Ltd* v *Cooley* [1972] 2 All ER 162.

39. Which of the following is NOT one of the duties of directors?

[A] A duty to act for proper purposes.
[B] A duty to act in the best interests of the board.
[C] A duty to have regard in the performance of their functions to the interests of the company's employees.
[D] A duty to act *bona fide* in the interest of the company.

40. Which of the following is NOT an exception to the prohibition on loans and related dealings with directors?

[A] A loan of £70,000 advanced by a money lending company to a director of that company at 1% below the interest rate offered to the general public.

[B] A loan by a company to the director of its holding company for the absolute sum of £3,000.

[C] The sum of £15,000 to directors of a company in order to meet transport and accommodation expenses of the business.

[D] A loan of £150,000 by an authorised bank to one of its directors on ordinary terms.

41. Which one of the following is NOT a characteristic of 'inside information' as defined by s. 56 of the Criminal Justice Act 1993?

[A] The information must be either specific or precise.

[B] The information must not have been made public.

[C] The information must relate to either securities or issuers in general.

[D] The information must be such that if it were made public, it would be likely to have a significant effect on the price of any securities.

42. David is a director of a company and he discloses information to Christopher about a secret takeover offer received by that company. Christopher immediately buys some shares in that company in anticipation of the announcement of the takeover and a subsequent rise in the share price of the company. Which of the following represents a defence to David in respect of the unauthorised disclosure of inside information?

[A] That at the time he believed on reasonable grounds that the information had been disclosed widely enough to ensure that none of those taking part in the dealing would be prejudiced by not having the information.

[B] That at the time he had reasonable grounds to believe that the person he disclosed the information to would advise others to deal but not personally deal in those securities.

[C] That at the time he disclosed the information he did not expect any person, because of the disclosure, to deal in the securities.

[D] That at the time he disclosed the information he did not expect any person, because of the disclosure, to deal in the securities, and that belief was based on reasonable grounds.

43. Which one of the following is NOT a characteristic of a floating charge?

[A] A charge on all of a class of assets of the company, present and future.

[B] A charge on a class of assets which in the ordinary course of a company's business would be changing from time to time.

[C] A charge which would allow the company to carry on its business in the ordinary way.

[D] A charge over an identifiable corporate asset yet to be acquired (i.e. future property).

44. X Co plc and its officers fail to register a floating charge created over its property in favour of Louise. Which of the following propositions apply to X Co plc and its officers?

[A] The officers only are liable to a fine.

[B] Both the company and its officers will be liable to a fine.

[C] The company only will be liable to a fine.

[D] Civil action only is available.

45. Which one of the following is NOT a consequence of a failure to register a charge within the initial 21-day period?

[A] The charge is void against the liquidation of the company.
[B] The charge is void against any person who for value has acquired an interest in the property subject to the charge.
[C] The obligation to repay the money secured by the charge is invalidated.
[D] The charge is void against any creditor of the company.

46. Which of the following circumstances will NOT provide for a floating charge to be invalidated under s. 245 of the Insolvency Act 1986?

[A] A charge created 8 months prior to insolvency in favour of a non-connected person and at that time the company was unable to pay its debts.
[B] A charge created 8 months prior to insolvency in favour of a non-connected person and as a result of that transaction the company was unable to pay its debts.
[C] A charge created 18 months prior to insolvency in favour of a shadow director of the company.
[D] A charge created 11 months prior to insolvency in favour of a non-connected person but the company was solvent at the time of making that transaction and remains so immediately following that transaction.

47. Glass Ltd wishes to purchase its own shares but is concerned to use the correct funds to do so. It does not have any distributable profits. Which of the following represents the correct advice to be given to Glass Ltd?

[A] The company can use capital to purchase the shares provided members agree to this.
[B] The company can use profits *only* to purchase the shares.
[C] The company can use capital to purchase the shares only if the court authorises this.
[D] Private companies are not permitted to purchase their own shares.

48. The decision in *Brady* v *Brady* [1989] AC 755 illustrates which of the following propositions?

[A] A company must always pay its dividends in cash.

[B] A company is not permitted directly to provide financial assistance for the acquisition of its own shares.

[C] A distinction must be drawn between a purpose of expenditure and the reason why a purpose was formed: the latter would be regarded as part of a larger purpose.

[D] The courts would always permit and recognise a larger purpose for expenditure, incorporating primary and secondary purposes.

49. Which of the following propositions represents the rule in *Foss* v *Harbottle* (1843) 2 Hare 461?

[A] Members can only complain to the court in situations involving procedural irregularities.

[B] The court will not interfere with the internal management of companies when directors are acting outside of their powers.

[C] It is the policy of the courts to refrain from hearing actions brought by members of the company when the wrong alleged is one done to the company.

[D] The will of the majority of the directors must always prevail.

50. Which of the following decisions is NOT an illustration of 'fraud on the minority'?

[A] *Daniels* v *Daniels* [1978] Ch 406.

[B] *Browne* v *La Trinidad* (1887) 37 ChD 1.

[C] *Estmanco (Kilner House) Ltd* v *Greater London Council* [1982] 1 All ER 437.

[D] *Cooke* v *Deeks and others* [1916] 1 AC 554.

51. In respect of an action under s. 459 of the Companies Act 1985, which of the following propositions is accurate?

[A] An action is available irrespective of whether the conduct affected members generally or some part of the membership only.

[B] An action will only be available where the conduct concerned the members interests as members and part only of the membership was affected.

[C] The conduct complained of must be shown to be objectively discriminatory and motivated by criminal intent.

[D] The conduct complained of must be shown to be motivated by malice and interferes with the personal and private rights of the members concerned.

52. Section 461(2) of the Companies Act 1985 provides a list of some examples of orders which are available. Which of the following orders is NOT included in s. 461(2)?

[A] An order to regulate the conduct of the company's affairs in the future.

[B] An order to require the company to refrain from doing an act complained of by the petitioner.

[C] An order to authorise civil proceedings to be brought in the name and on behalf of the company by such persons as the court may direct.

[D] An order to disqualify officers of the company from acting directly or indirectly in the promotion or future management of that company or related companies.

53. In *Ebrahimi* v *Westbourne Galleries* [1973] AC 360, Lord Wilberforce identified a number of circumstances where it might be appropriate for a court to depart from adhering to the strict legal rights of membership and consider winding up of the company on the grounds that it is just and equitable to do so. Which one of the following was NOT part of Lord Wilberforce's suggestions?

[A]   Where a company was formed or continued on the basis of a personal relationship which involved mutual confidence.

[B]   If there was an agreement or understanding that all or some of the members of the company would be responsible for the management of the company.

[C]   Where there was a restriction on the transfer of a member's interest in the company so that if confidence is lost, or one member is removed from management, he cannot take out his stake and go elsewhere.

[D]   Where the company is a private company whose main object can no longer be achieved.

54. For the members of a company to commence its voluntary winding up they must adopt a resolution that the company be wound up (Insolvency Act 1986, s. 84(1)). Which one of the following resolutions is NOT available to commence a company's winding up?

[A]   An extraordinary resolution where members have lost confidence in the company's board of directors.

[B]   A special resolution that the company be wound up in order to give effect to a scheme of arrangements.

[C]   An extraordinary resolution where it is apparent that, by reason of its liabilities, the company cannot continue its business.

[D]   An ordinary resolution where the articles of the company provide that it should cease operations on the expiry of a certain time limit which has now expired.

55. Ian is a director of Holmes plc and it is believed that he has been involved in causing the company to continue in business knowing that the company was unable to pay its debts. Ian has also been involved in diverting business away from Holmes plc to his own wholly owned single member private limited company. Which of the following statutory provisions are likely to apply to Ian's situation?

[A] Section 214 of the Insolvency Act 1986 only.
[B] Sections 213 and 212 of the Insolvency Act 1986.
[C] Sections 213 and 214 of the Insolvency Act 1986.
[D] Sections 214 and 212 of the Insolvency Act 1986.

56. Under s. 432(2) of the Companies Act 1985 the Secretary of State enjoys a discretion, in certain circumstances, to order an investigation of a company's affairs. Which one of the following matters is NOT included in s. 432(2) as a ground for the exercise of that discretion?

[A] A belief that the company's affairs have been conducted with an intent to defraud creditors.
[B] A belief that the company was formed for any fraudulent or unlawful purpose.
[C] A belief that the company has failed to achieve its objects.
[D] A belief that shareholders have not been given all the information with respect to the management of a company's affairs which they might reasonably have expected to have been given.

57. Jet Ltd has recently offered to purchase shares in Wing Ltd and 90% of members have accepted Jet's offer. Tom initially rejected Jet Ltd's offer, but has now changed his mind and wishes to sell his shares to Jet Ltd. Which of the following represents the correct advice to Tom?

[A] Having rejected Jet's initial offer, Tom must now seek another purchaser for his shares.
[B] Because Jet Ltd has now acquired 90% of shares in Wing Ltd, Tom can insist that Wing Ltd purchase his shares at a price agreed through an independent valuation.
[C] Tom must approach Jet Ltd and ask them to make a fresh offer to purchase his shares.
[D] Tom can give notice to Jet Ltd and insist that they purchase his shares on the same terms as the original offer.

58. Companies wishing to make a distribution must comply with statutory rules seeking to ensure that it is only accumulated, realised profits, that are used. These rules apply to 'every description of distribution of a company's assets to its members, whether in cash or otherwise' (s. 263(2) of the Companies Act 1985), subject to a number of exceptions. Which one of the following is NOT an exception?

[A] The return of capital to members in a properly authorised reduction of capital.
[B] The sale at undervalue of an asset by a company to its sole beneficial shareholder.
[C] The issue of fully or partly paid bonus shares.
[D] The purchase or redemption of the company's own shares.

59. The decision in *R v Panel on Takeovers & Mergers, ex parte Datafin plc* [1987] QB 815 illustrates which one of the following propositions?

[A] Decisions by the City Panel on Takeovers and Mergers cannot be challenged in the courts.
[B] The courts are willing to overrule and reverse decisions of the City Panel.
[C] The courts are inclined to give declarations of the meaning of rules in the City Code on Takeovers and Mergers for future guidance rather than reverse past decisions of the City Panel.
[D] The courts may disagree with the City Panel's interpretation of the City Code in order to prevent unwanted takeovers and mergers.

60. Which of the following rules does the City Code on Takeovers and Mergers consist of?

[A] Rules and principles to promote good business conduct during takeovers and mergers.
[B] Statutory rules regulating directors conduct during takeovers and mergers.
[C] The voluntary acceptance of competition law principles.
[D] A voluntary acceptance of the legal rights attached to shares.

APPENDIX 1

ANSWERS TO MCT1

1.	B	16.	C	31.	C	46.	D
2.	C	17.	A	32.	B	47.	C
3.	B	18.	B	33.	C	48.	B
4.	D	19.	D	34.	C	49.	A
5.	A	20.	A	35.	C	50.	A
6.	D	21.	C	36.	A	51.	B
7.	C	22.	A	37.	B	52.	D
8.	A	23.	D	38.	A	53.	C
9.	A	24.	B	39.	D	54.	D
10.	B	25.	D	40.	B	55.	B
11.	C	26.	C	41.	B	56.	A
12.	D	27.	A	42.	D	57.	D
13.	D	28.	C	43.	C	58.	C
14.	D	29.	B	44.	A	59.	B
15.	C	30.	C	45.	B	60.	D

APPENDIX 2

ANSWERS TO MCT2

1.	A	16.	B	31.	A	46.	D
2.	C	17.	D	32.	C	47.	A
3.	D	18.	C	33.	A	48.	C
4.	C	19.	B	34.	B	49.	C
5.	D	20.	C	35.	D	50.	B
6.	B	21.	A	36.	B	51.	A
7.	C	22.	D	37.	A	52.	D
8.	A	23.	C	38.	D	53.	D
9.	C	24.	B	39.	B	54.	A
10.	B	25.	B	40.	A	55.	D
11.	D	26.	B	41.	C	56.	C
12.	D	27.	C	42.	C	57.	D
13.	C	28.	C	43.	D	58.	B
14.	D	29.	A	44.	B	59.	C
15.	A	30.	C	45.	C	60.	A

APPENDIX 3

NOTE-FORM ANSWERS TO MCT1

1. Answer [B] is *advantageous*. Statements i, ii and iii are all correct statements about a partnership. However, joint and several liability for business debts is in fact a disadvantage making [A], [C] and [D] incorrect. A partnership is created by agreement between the partners. Every partner in a partnership is liable for all debts and obligations of the firm incurred whilst he/she is a partner (s. 9 of the Partnership Act 1890). There is no limit on a partner's liability for the firm's debts and obligations. A partnership does not constitute a separate legal entity as opposed to a company which is a separate legal entity. Companies limited by shares have the advantage of offering shareholders limited liability. One disadvantage of incorporation is that certain information has to be disclosed to the Registrar of Companies and is available to the public. Statement iv is not strictly correct as any tax rates depend on the income of the individuals concerned.

2. Answer [C] is correct. Shareholders' liability is limited to the fully paid up nominal value of the shares held. Shareholders who have only partly paid for their shares will be liable to pay the balance outstanding on their shares. The advantages of trading as a company limited by shares are demonstrated by the case of *Salomon v A Salomon & Co. Ltd* [1897] AC 22. The justification for allowing companies to have limited liability is that it encourages people to invest in business. However, limited liability has obvious risks for business creditors who may not be paid in full the amount of money owing to them. [A] is incorrect because the shareholders have the benefit of limited liability (as set out in [C]). [B] is incorrect because if shares are not fully paid up, the shareholders are liable up to the fully paid up nominal value of their shares. [D] is incorrect because liability is limited as in [C] and shareholders are not liable for the total debts of the company.

3. All these statements about a company are correct; however only [B] is an advantage. The benefit of limited liability is often the main reason that businesses seek incorporation. Perpetual succession [A] means that the company continues even where the individual directors have ceased to exist. The company is a separate legal entity. As such it is entitled to hold property in the name of the company. Disclosure of corporate matters to the Registrar of Companies ([C]) may well be a disadvantage.

4. Answer [D] is the only answer which is actually INCORRECT. The veil is not only lifted where there is fraud or illegality although it is one example of when the courts will look at the reality of the situation and may disregard the veil of incorporation. See, for example, *Jones v Lipman* [1963] 1 WLR 832 where the company was being used to avoid a personal obligation. The veil can also be lifted by statute, for example, tax legislation or s. 214, Insolvency Act 1986. [A] can be illustrated by *Creasey v Breachwood Motors Limited* [1992] BCC 678 where a company transferred all its assets to another company to avoid its legal obligations in pending litigation. [B] can be illustrated by the same case where the court indicated that a decision would depend on the actual circumstances of each case and therefore would be difficult to predict. [C] is a correct statement of the recently decided cases on groups of companies where the separate legal personality of the companies within a group is maintained: see *Adams v Cape Industries plc* [1990] Ch 433, CA.

5. Answer [A] is correct and DOES NOT support the proposition. In *DHN Food Distributors Limited v Tower Hamlets London Borough Council* [1976] 1 WLR 852 the courts looked at the reality of the situation and decided that the separate legal personality of the companies in the group could not be maintained and that the group of companies should be treated as an economic entity. In this case DHN Food Distributors Limited was the holding company of a group of three companies. One of the wholly-owned subsidiaries owned freehold land which was used by the holding company but not by the subsidiary. On the compulsory purchase of the land the holding company claimed compensation for disturbance of its business. This claim was upheld in the Court of Appeal. Mr Woolfson in *Woolfson* v *Strathclyde Regional Council* 1978 SLT 159 ([B]) tried to rely on this case to pursue his claim for compensation against the local council but failed in the House of Lords. More recent cases as in [C] and [D] seem to have treated groups of companies as comprising a number of companies which are to be treated as separate legal entities and have not followed the *DHN* case.

6. Answer [D] is correct. The order for payment of creditors is secured creditors, costs of liquidation, preferential creditors, unsecured creditors and postponed creditors. Anything remaining is then returned to the creditors. As a debenture holder Jonah is a secured creditor and will be paid in preference to ordinary trade creditors or creditors with a floating charge over the company assets. His security may be subordinated to other secured creditors and in any event will only be repaid if the company has sufficient assets to pay the value of the security. The facts in this example are very similar to those in *Salomon* v *Salomon* [1897] AC 22 (see answer 2 above). Under s. 154, Insolvency Act 1986 all creditors are to be paid equally subject to: (a) payment of expenses (*Batten* v *Wedgewood Coal and Iron Co.* (1884) 28 ChD 317); (b) preferential debts (ss. 175, 386, 387 and sch. 6, Insolvency Act 1986); (c) principles of set off (r. 4.90, Insolvency Rules 1986). These principles determine the order of priority of payment.

7. Answer [C] is correct. Section 14(1) of the Companies Act 1985 states that:

> Subject to the provisions of this Act, the memorandum and articles when registered bind the company and its members to the same extent as if they respectively had been signed and sealed by each member and contained covenants on the part of each member to observe all the provisions of the memorandum and of the articles.

The effect of the s. 14 contract is that the memorandum and articles constitute a contract between the members and the company and between the members *inter se*. There is academic debate about the ability of a member to enforce rights as an outsider: see Wedderburn [1957] CLJ 194, Goldberg (1972) 35 MLR 362, Prentice (1980) 1 Co

Law 179. Arguably s. 14 refers to all rights under the contract but the courts have chosen to give the section the selective meaning in [C]. [A] and [B] are not enforced by the courts and s. 14 makes no mention of a 2-year qualifying period ([D]). For a good explanation of the s. 14 contract see the article by Robert Gregory (1981) 44 MLR 526.

8. Answer [A] is correct. These facts are similar to the facts in the case of *Quin & Axtens Ltd* v *Salmon* [1909] AC 442. If this case were to be followed Kenneth would be able to enforce the terms of the articles in his capacity as a member of the company although this would have the effect of enforcing rights conferred upon him in his capacity as a director. [D] is incorrect because he cannot enforce rights under the articles in his capacity as a director of the company. [B] is incorrect as many commentators have argued that a member can enforce rights other than those which only affect him as a member. The reasons for such views may differ. For instance, Goldberg (1972) 35 MLR 362 argues that a member can insist on the affairs of the company being conducted as stated in the articles. Wedderburn [1957] CLJ 194 argues that a member can indirectly enforce outsider rights if he is both a member and an outsider. Since [A] is correct [C] cannot also be correct.

9. Answer [A] is correct. Answer [C] is incorrect although a company needs to pass a special resolution to amend its articles under s. 9 of the Companies Act 1985. There are restrictions imposed on the ability of a company to amend its articles which are set out in s. 16 of the Companies Act 1985. A further restriction imposed is that the power to alter a company's articles must be exercised *bona fide* for the benefit of the company as a whole: *Allen* v *Gold Reefs of West Africa Ltd* [1900] 1 Ch 956. Therefore alteration by special resolution will not automatically be valid. [B] is incorrect because if the alteration was intended to apply indiscriminately to all members, the alteration cannot be challenged: *Greenhalgh* v *Arderne Cinemas Ltd* [1951] Ch 286. [D] is incorrect because the court will generally accept the majority's view of whether the alteration is for the benefit of the company as a whole provided that a reasonable person could consider the alteration for the benefit of the company: *Shuttleworth* v *Cox Bros & Co. (Maidenhead) Ltd* [1927] 2 KB 9. Therefore Beatrice and Candide will have to demonstrate that the alteration is for the benefit of the company as a whole.

10. Answer [B] is correct. See *Hickman v Kent and Romney Marsh Sheep-Breeders' Association* [1915] 1 Ch 881 where Mr Hickman was a member of the Association. The Association tried to expel him and Mr Hickman brought an injunction against the Association although there was a provision in the articles that all disputes be referred to arbitration. The Association could enforce a stay on the injunction because Mr Hickman was not acting in accordance with the provisions of the articles of association. Accordingly, answers [A], [C] and [D] are incorrect since neither David nor Bertrand is given powers of dispute resolution under the articles of association.

11. Answer [C] is correct. Accordingly answer [A] is incorrect. Under s. 36(4) of the Companies Act 1985 an individual who enters into a pre-incorporation contract, which is what this contract is, will be personally liable for the contract. Jane could try to negotiate with the office supplier for the contract for which she is personally liable to be novated to the company when it is incorporated. The supplier will not be bound to agree to this novation of the contract. Jane should have either waited until the company was incorporated or informed the supplier of the problem and ensured as in answer [B] that they would agree to a novation of the contract after the formation of the company. [B] is correct but does not deal with the question of Jane's liability which is personal liability. As Jane herself is liable the supplier has no action against J & I Designs Limited ([D]).

12. Answer [D] is correct. The *ultra vires* rule was established in *Ashbury Railway Carriage & Iron Co. Ltd v Riche* (1857) LR 7 HL 653. Any act which was *ultra vires* the company's memorandum was beyond its capacity and void. Such an *ultra vires* action it was held in this case could not be ratified even by a unanimous decision of the shareholders. This rule has now been abolished by the Companies Act 1989 inserting a new s. 35(1) into the Companies Act 1985. Statements [A], [B] and [C] are true but are not found in *Ashbury Railway Carriage*. [C] may have been a correct view of the memorandum in the 19th century but is no longer realistic as a result of the changes to the *ultra vires* rule introduced by the amendments to s. 35 of the Companies Act 1985.

13. Answer [D] is correct. The new s. 35 of the Companies Act 1985 retains some measure of protection for the members of a company in that they can prevent the directors entering into certain future transactions which would normally be valid due to the effect of s. 35(1). This may be seen as a kind of compromise in that both third parties who contract with the company and the members are protected in the situation where directors enter into *ultra vires* transactions. [A] is incorrect because the shareholders can only prevent the directors entering into a contract in the future and this is dependant on the shareholders knowing what the directors plan to do. The effect of s. 35(1) is that an outsider dealing with the company is not at risk even if the company is acting outside its powers under the memorandum. [B] is incorrect because the protection for third parties under s. 35 only applies where the company has acted ultra vires, it is irrelevant whether the transaction has been approved by all the directors [C].

14. Answer [D] is correct. As the loan was taken out after 1992 it would be governed by s. 35, Companies Act 1985 and under s. 35(1) the validity of an act done by a company shall not be called into question by reason of anything in the company's memorandum ([A]). Therefore the only requirement to test the validity of the loan would be that it was validly executed. The other tests of acting in good faith ([B]) and the directors acting in the best interests of the company ([C]) are no longer necessary under the Companies Act 1989.

15. Answer [C] is correct. Before the Companies Act 1989 came into operation different tests were imposed to test the validity of transactions. The additional objects clause is a subjective objects clause like the one in *Bell Houses Ltd* v *City Wall Properties Ltd* [1966] 2 QB 656. It authorises the directors to enter into transactions which they believe are in the best interests of the company. Therefore, the loan would be an authorised transaction and could be enforced by the bank and so answer [A] is incorrect. The requirement of good faith was not necessary ([B]) nor that the contract was validly executed ([D]). The answer would be different before 1989 although the contract would still be valid.

16. There has been much debate as to whether the shareholders could interfere in the management of the company by ordinary resolution. It was confirmed in *Breckland Group Holdings Ltd* v *London & Suffolk Properties Ltd* [1989] BCLC 100 that the general meeting can only interfere with the board's exercise of the power of management by special resolution ([A]). However, a company can distribute the powers of management as it wishes by adopting a form of articles which changes the effect of Article 70, Table A which gives general powers of management to the directors ([D]). Also, under s. 303 of the Companies Act 1985 members have a statutory right to dismiss a director by ordinary resolution ([B]). Therefore, statement [C] is the only one which is INCORRECT.

17. Answer [A] is the correct advice. Although all the other statements are true, Norman should be advised of his duties as a director of the company. Even though he is a non-executive director English company law does not recognise any distinction between an executive and a non-executive director. In order to ensure that he is able to do the job properly and to protect himself he should ensure that he is given sufficient information, particularly financial and management information, about the company. As a non-executive director Norman will owe the same standard of care to the company and the shareholders as if he were an executive director.

18. Answer [B] is correct. The definition of a shadow director in s. 741 of the Companies Act 1985 is 'A person in accordance with whose directions or instructions the directors of a company are deemed to act'. Margaret is clearly acting as a shadow director and could be held to be in breach of duties owed to the company and shareholders. [D] is incorrect since although the other directors know what is going on and could be held equally responsible for breach of their duties, Margaret may have liability in her role as shadow director. [A] is incorrect as Margaret will not have liability solely in her role as a shareholder because she is acting as a shadow director. Answer [C] is incorrect because the shareholders do not have equal shareholdings and Margaret may be personally liable for her actions as a shadow director if they involve the company in loss.

19. Answer [D] is correct. Subject to Article 82 of Table A an increase in salary will be permitted provided that it is approved by the company in general meeting. However, directors should be aware that large salary increases may only lead to problems in the future for the company if the company does not have sufficient funds to pay for these increases. [A] is incorrect because increases in directors' salaries need to be approved in general meeting. [B] is incorrect because although the effect of excessive salaries may be as stated it does not follow that directors may not increase their salaries. [C] is correct but does not affect the issue of salary increase and is not relevant to Jill's query.

20. [A] is the correct answer. You are asked about the best way to protect each of the sisters from being removed as a director and this would be to insert a *Bushell v Faith* clause from the case of *Bushell v Faith* [1970] AC 1099 where the House of Lords upheld weighted voting rights for directors when a resolution was proposed to remove a director. Answer [B] is a possibility but [A] is better and could be included in the articles of association. Answer [C] is incorrect as each sister cannot have a majority shareholding. A long term service contract would not prevent any of the sisters from being dismissed but may give them a right to compensation for breach of contract.

21. Answer [C] is correct. The rule in *Foss v Harbottle* (1843) 2 Hare 461 is that where a wrong has been suffered by a company the company is the proper plaintiff to bring any action against the wrongdoer. The rationale is therefore made up of statements ii, iii, and iv. Statement i is found in *Salomon v Salomon & Co. Ltd* [1897] AC 22. There are exceptions to this rule to prevent injustice where the wrongdoers are in control of operating the company. The main reasons for the rule are that the court is not interested in hearing actions brought by an individual concerning company matters unless one of the exceptions to the rule applies.

22. Answers [B], [C] and [D] are correct statements of the grounds that a minority shareholder must establish before bringing a derivative action. Answer [A] is therefore INCORRECT. The exception to the rule in *Foss v Harbottle* (1843) 2 Hare 461 requires there to have been a fraud perpetrated against the minority shareholders not against the company. The fraud complained of need not be confined to literal or common law fraud and the shareholder need not always allege fraud.

23. [D] is the correct answer and the most appropriate action for Frances to take. [A] is incorrect because her action would not be representative of the other members of the company as there are no other members who need to take any action. [B] is incorrect as her action is not a personal action arising out of a breach of the articles. There is no contractual right under the articles for the payment of a dividend. [C] is incorrect because Frances wishes the company to remain in existence. Following *Burland* v *Earle* [1902] AC 83, a shareholder has no right to sue for payment of a dividend unless it has been declared. Frances is alleging fraud on the minority. The grounds for her allegation are that the directors are not distributing profits to the shareholders but are paying to themselves large directors' fees since she knows that the company has been profitable for the last three years.

24. [B] is the correct answer as a shareholder has no right to be appointed as a director of a company. [A] is a situation where the court has allowed a petition for unfairly prejudicial conduct under s. 459 of the Companies Act 1985: see *Re Cumana Ltd* [1986] BCLC 430. In this case it was well known by the majority that a rights issue on favourable terms to the shareholders could not be taken up by a minority shareholder. [C] is similar to the case of *Re Sam Weller & Sons Ltd* [1990] BCLC 80 where the dividend payments had not increased over 37 years despite the company being successful. This failure to pay an appropriate level of dividend affected all shareholders (not only minority shareholders) but was held to be unfairly prejudicial conduct. The amendments to s. 459 made by the Companies Act 1989, sch. 19 para. 11, would also make such conduct unfairly prejudicial even if it did not affect all members. [D] is similar to the case of *Re a Company (No. 003160 of 1986)* [1986] BCLC 391 where the exclusion from management of a minority shareholder was held to be unfairly prejudicial conduct.

25. Answer [D] is correct. [C] is not a possible remedy set out in s. 461 of the Companies Act 1985. [A] is one of the possible remedies set out in s. 461(2)(d) of the Companies Act 1985. [B] is the power given to the court set out in s. 461(1) of the Companies Act 1985. [D] is the power given to the court under s. 461(2)(a) of the Companies Act 1985. If an order is made for the purchase of the minority shareholders' shares, the minority shareholder can request a valuation by the court if there is a risk of undervaluation in the articles of association – *Re a Company (No. 00330 of 1991)* [1991] BCLC 597.

26. Answer [C] is correct. Although Hilary is in breach of her duty of confidentiality which she owes to her employer the only offences which she has committed under the Criminal Justice Act 1993 are encouraging to deal (statement ii) by encouraging Isobel to sell all her shares in the company and disclosing information (statement iv) by disclosing this confidential price sensitive information to Isobel. Although she is a primary insider (statement i), as she obtained the information by virtue of her employment, this is not an offence. Hilary may be guilty of professional misconduct as she owes a duty of confidentiality to her employer and to Cumbrae plc (statement iii) but this is not an offence under the Act.

27. Answer [A] is correct. Isobel has got her information from Hilary who is a primary insider and has then dealt in shares. [B] is incorrect as Isobel is not in the position of a primary insider under s. 57(2)(a), Criminal Justice Act 1993. [C] and [D] are both incorrect because Isobel does not tell anyone else about her inside information nor does she encourage anyone else to deal in shares.

28. Answer [C] is correct. Greg is a secondary insider as he got his information from the Managing Director of Cumbrae plc or in the course of his employment. However, he may have a defence under s. 53(1)(a), Criminal Justice Act 1993 if he could show that he would have sold the shares anyway due to pressing financial hardship. [A] is incorrect because he is not a primary insider. [B] is incorrect because Greg has received information from an inside source. [D] is incorrect as he does not encourage anyone else to deal in securities.

29. Answer [B] is correct. Statements ii and iii, in [A], [C] and [D], are irrelevant because no offence is committed under s. 57(1) of the Criminal Justice Act 1993 unless the company in which there has been insider dealing is a quoted company (statement iv). However, Fiona has clearly breached the duty of confidentiality owed to her employer as it is unlikely that this information should have been divulged (statement i).

30. Answer [C] is correct. The definition of having information as an insider is that the information is inside information (statement i) and that the individual knows that it is inside information and knows it is from an inside source (statement iii). Statement ii is only part of the definition of inside information. Intention is not relevant to the definition of having information as an insider (statement iv).

31. Answer [C] is correct. [A] and [D] are also true but are not relevant to Basil Limited. The charge needs to be registered within the requisite time period to be valid and also is only valid in respect of fresh consideration issued after granting the charge and not in respect of past indebtedness. The order of priority of payments on a liquidation is: secured creditors, costs of liquidation, preferential creditors, floating charges, ordinary creditors. (See answer to question 6 for principles determining the order of priority of payment of debts.)

32. Answer [B] is correct. Under s. 214 of the Insolvency Act 1986 wrongful trading applies when a director knew or ought to have concluded that insolvent liquidation was unavoidable. The difficulty occurs in ascertaining the actual knowledge which the director had or ought to have had at a particular time. If a director has a particular skill, for example, as a finance director, a higher standard will be expected of that person with regard to the finances of the company than from a director without any specific financial expertise. [A] is incorrect because the test is not that of a reasonable person but someone in the director's position with her knowledge. [C] is incorrect – this test is the minimal test imposed on directors generally and has no relevance to s. 214 of the Insolvency Act 1986. [D] is incorrect because it does not state any standard which should be imposed. The test under s. 214 of the Insolvency Act 1986 has been clarified in recent case law: *Re Produce Marketing Consortium Limited (No. 2)* [1989] BCLC 520.

33. Answer [C] is correct. An unsecured creditor will only be paid if the other creditor ranking ahead of that creditor has been paid in full. See answer 6 above for order of priority of payment of creditors on a liquidation.

34. Answer [C] is correct. An administrative receiver is appointed by a creditor with a floating charge over the assets of a company (statement ii). The purpose of their appointment is to realise sufficient assets to satisfy the creditor's floating charge (statement iv). The power to appoint an administrative receiver is contained in the floating charge agreement. In contrast, an administrator is appointed pursuant to an application to court under ss. 8–27 of the Insolvency Act 1986 (statement i). Once appointed there is a moratorium of 3 months on actions by creditors to recover assets, whereas statement iii says nothing about a moratorium. The court cannot make an administration order if an administrative receiver has been appointed.

35. Answer [C] is correct. There is an easier burden of proof in the concept of wrongful trading as opposed to fraudulent trading as there is no requirement to show intention to defraud creditors. However, unless there has been clear irresponsibility on the part of the directors and the director has substantial assets there is little point in the liquidator pursuing such a director. It can be very difficult to ascertain exactly when the directors should have realised that liquidation would be unavoidable. It is of course easier to ascertain this after the event. See *Re Purpoint Ltd* [1991] BCC 121 and *Re Produce Marketing Consortium Ltd (No. 2)* [1989] BCLC 520. [A] is a correct statement but this does not create a problem as there is a lower burden of proof for a civil offence than for a criminal offence. [B] is a correct statement but again it is not a problem as it is easier to show wrongful trading than to establish the necessary intention to defraud for fraudulent trading. [D] is incorrect because the test imposed is both subjective and objective.

36. Answer [A] is correct. Denis could bring an action for unfairly prejudicial conduct as he is in the majority and has been excluded from the decision. Answer [B] is incorrect because it details action which can be taken by the company and not by Denis. [C] is incorrect because it makes no difference that the contract may have been offered to Derek and Ken due to their skills in the hotel trade: see *IDC* v *Cooley* [1972] 1 WLR 443. [D] is incorrect because *Queensland Mines Ltd* v *Hudson* (1978) 52 AJLR and *Peso Silver Mines Ltd* v *Cropper* (1966) 58 DLR (2d) 1, suggest that a director may take up a contract if the board have decided to reject the contract.

37. Answer [B] is correct. It is impossible to say that he will be unable to vote without looking at the articles of association of the company. However, if there are provisions similar to Articles 94 and

95 of Table A he will be unable to vote or form part of the quorum on the resolution to approve this contract because of his personal interest ([A]). Without looking at the articles the only thing that it is possible to say is that under s. 317 of the Companies Act 1985 he must declare his personal interest in this contract at the first board meeting at which it is raised. Provided that he does this he will owe no further duties to the company and he need take no further action, in particular he has no need to resign ([C]). A failure to comply with s. 317 means that he will be liable to a fine. Taking no action as in [D] is not permissible.

38. Answer [A] is correct. Regardless of their actual knowledge Martha and Mary will be liable for wrongful trading on the basis that they should have been aware of financial matters in their capacity as directors. The objective standard under s. 214(4) of the Insolvency Act 1986 will apply to them both. Both Martha and Mary will be liable for wrongful trading even though Mary has no financial expertise, or been involved in the financial aspects of the company ([C]). [B] is correct but an incomplete statement as Martha alone will not have to contribute to the company's assets. [D] is incorrect — unless fraud can be shown, Martha will not face criminal liability for fraudulent trading.

39. Answer [D] is correct. See *Neptune (Vehicle Washing Equipment) Ltd v Fitzgerald (No. 2)* [1995] 3 WLR 108 where the defendant was a sole director. Lightman J said that even if holding a meeting on his/her own a sole director must have a statutory pause for thought and record disclosure of his/her interest in the minutes. If a company secretary is present the declaration should be made aloud. If the articles permit a director to have an interest in a contract subject to disclosure then failure to disclose will amount to breach of duty whereby the contract will be voidable at the company's option. The director must declare his/her interest and state the nature of that interest. Subject to this declaration (s. 317, Companies Act 1985) the termination payment to Candide will be valid. [B] is therefore incorrect as even sole directors must declare interests, but failure to disclose will not render the payment voidable ([A]). [C] is irrelevant.

40. Answer [B] is correct. There has been an issue of shares for an improper purpose (statement i) (*Howard Smith Limited v Ampol*

Petroleum Ltd [1974] 2 WLR 689) and a substantial property transaction to a director in breach of s. 320 of the Companies Act 1985 (statement ii). The effect of this is that the contract for the sale of the car to Michelle may be voidable (statement iii) and if Paul and Michelle colluded they may be liable to compensate the company for any loss suffered (statement iv). We do not know if there are any other shareholders or directors in the company involved in these transactions.

41. Answer [B] is correct. [A] is in effect someone who is a *de facto* director – they act as if they were a director but have not been validly appointed. [C] is a definition of an ordinary *de jure* director. Professional advisers are specifically excluded from the definition of shadow director ([D]). Answer 18 above gives the definition of a shadow director.

42. Answer [D] is correct. Companies within a group structure are treated for legal purposes as separate legal entities and the holding company has no legal liability for the debts of the subsidiary company. [B] is also a correct statement of the English company law treatment of groups of companies but is not a statement of the liability which ABC plc will have for any compensation claims. [A] is not correct and only in the case of *DHN Food Distributors Ltd* v *Tower Hamlets London Borough Council* [1976] 1 WLR 852 has this been the position. [C] is incorrect as companies within a group are usually treated as separate legal entities and the parent company has no responsibility for the liabilities of its subsidiaries.

43. Answer [C] is correct. [A] is incorrect because there is an essential difference in the way that a group is treated for tax and accounting purposes – a group is treated largely as a single unit for tax purposes which leads to no taxation of intragroup transactions. A group has to prepare group accounts. For some other purposes, for example, directors' interests, the existence of a group of companies can be relevant but not for the purposes of limited liability. The treatment for tax and accounting purposes is to look at the reality of the situation but this has not been carried forward into the treatment of groups generally. [B] is incorrect because for legal purposes companies within a group are treated as separate legal entities but for tax and accounting purposes the group is treated as one entity. [D] is incorrect as there are other examples of lifting the veil.

44. Answer [A] is correct. The rule in *Turquand's* case (*Royal British Bank* v *Turquand* (1856) 6 E & B 327) states that a third party can rely on the fact that the required internal rules have been followed (statement i). Timber Limited will be aware of the provisions of the articles but there are no public documents showing whether the ordinary resolution has been passed. The effect of s. 35A of the Companies Act 1985 is that third parties should not be prejudiced when entering into contracts with a company by virtue of limitations under the company's constitution (statement ii). The contract will therefore be valid and enforceable by Timber Limited. Statement iii is incorrect because the contract will be binding irrespective of ratification: see (i) above. Statement iv is incorrect as this test is not applicable under s. 35A of the Companies Act 1985.

45. Answer [B] is correct. [A] is incorrect because even though Marilyn has no actual authority she may have apparent authority particularly if she has bought tickets before, although Sadlers Wells should have been alerted by the size of the purchase. Answer [C] is incorrect because her personal liability cannot be established on the information available. [D] is incorrect because it would not be obvious that she would have no authority to enter into this kind of transaction.

46. Answer [D] is correct. The facts in this question are similar to those in *Hogg* v *Cramphorn Limited* [1967] 3 All ER 420. Although in that case the directors honestly believed the proposed takeover was in the best interests of the company it was held that the power to issue shares had been exercised for an improper purpose, namely, to prevent a takeover. The proper purpose for which shares should be issued is to raise capital. This approach was also taken in *Howard Smith Limited* v *Ampol Petroleum Limited* [1974] AC 821 where shares were issued to reduce the holding of a shareholder. The issue of shares in that case was also held to be for an improper purpose and therefore void. The improper purpose rule applies even if the directors are acting in the best interests of the company. [A] is incorrect because the directors are acting in good faith – this is not the reason why the share issue can be challenged. [B] is incorrect as this is not the effect of improperly issued shares. The validity of the share issue can be challenged on the grounds set out in [D] but the issue is not automatically invalid. [C] is incorrect because this is not relevant to the allotment of shares.

47. Answer [C] is correct. The facts in this example are similar to those in *Aberdeen Railway Co.* v *Blaikie Brothers* [1843–60] All ER Rep 249, HL. In this case the railway company contracted to buy chairs from a partnership. One of the directors of the railway company was also a member of the partnership. It was held that the contract was voidable because of the director's conflict of interest. Where directors have such a conflict of interest they should declare that interest at any board meeting where the contract in which they have an interest is discussed. [A] is incorrect because the contract is voidable and therefore the partnership is not entitled to payment. [C] is incorrect as it is not the reason why contract is unenforceable. [D] is incorrect in relation to this contract and is irrelevant.

48. Answer [B] is correct. Section 320 of the Companies Act 1985 makes substantial property transactions between a director and the company illegal and voidable if they are not first approved by the company in general meeting. A substantial property transaction is one which involves a non-cash asset of the requisite value being sold by a director to the company or bought by a director from the company. Requisite value is defined as an asset which exceeds the lesser of £100,000 or 10% of the company's net assets. An agreement entered into in contravention of s. 320 is generally voidable at the instance of the company. This is a substantial property transaction because it is worth 15% of the company's net assets. [A] is incorrect as the requirement for approval under s. 320 is in addition to a directors duty to declare their interest in a contract under s. 317 of the Companies Act 1985. [C] is incorrect as the contract is voidable *not* void. [D] is incorrect because we cannot predict whether Mary's action will lead to her removal as a director.

49. Answer [A] is correct. A contract which has a term in excess of 5 years which has not been approved by the company in general meeting will be valid except for the provision relating to the term of the contract. [B] is not correct as proof of gross misconduct is not necessary. The company will be able to terminate the contract on reasonable notice under s. 319 of the Companies Act 1985 regardless of conduct. There have been recommendations by the Cadbury Report (Report of the Committee on the Financial Aspects of Corporate Governance 1992) to reduce the maximum length of directors' service contracts to 3 years although this has been followed by many listed companies it has not yet been enshrined in statute. [C] is incorrect because approval is needed by the company in general meeting and not by the directors. [D] is incorrect because the failure to have the contract approved means it can be terminated on reasonable notice.

50. Answer [A] is correct. Leo will not necessarily have the right to compensation as in [B], but may have the right to compensation for dismissal before the end of the term of his service contract depending on its terms. [C] is incorrect since under Table A there are no weighted voting rights for directors on their removal from office, such weighted voting rights would have to be included separately in a so-called *Bushell* v *Faith* clause. A director with no such weighted voting rights and also with less than 50% of the voting rights is in a vulnerable position if the majority shareholders decide to dismiss him under s. 303 of the Companies Act 1985. A director who is to be dismissed in this way has certain rights namely to be notified of the meeting and to represent himself at the general meeting which is voting on his removal. [D] is good advice but comes too late to save Leo.

51. Answer [B] is correct. There is a general prohibition against a company giving financial assistance for the purchase of its own shares contained in s. 151 of the Companies Act 1985. However certain exceptions are allowed for both public and private companies none of which apply here. Finally, private companies can go through the whitewash procedure which has the effect of authorising financial assistance provided that the strict procedural requirements are satisfied. As Falconer is a private company limited by shares Magna will be able to use this whitewash procedure and use Falconer's assets to secure the loan. [A] is correct but may be mitigated if Falconer follows the requisite procedural requirements. [C] is incorrect because it is not relevant to the use of assets here. [D] is not correct because a private company may also use the whitewash procedure set out in ss. 155–158 of the Companies Act 1985.

52. Answer [D] is correct. Statement i is clearly financial assistance for purchase of own shares by the parent which is prohibited.

Statement iv is also a clear example of financial assistance. Statement ii is not financial assistance because it is assets rather than shares which are being purchased and iii is an exception to the rule under s. 153(3)(a) of the Companies Act 1985.

53. Answer [C] is correct. The decision whether to declare a dividend is made by the directors of a company but [A] is incorrect as this decision is then voted on by the members at a general meeting of the company. However members cannot declare a larger dividend than the directors have suggested. Under s. 263 of the Companies Act 1985 dividends can only be paid out of profits available. To decide whether there are profits available the directors must deduct from all the realised profits all the realised losses to date. If there is any profit left after doing that then money is available to pay a dividend as it is in this example. Contrary to [D] there is no distinction between income and capital profits. [B] is incorrect because the rules on payment of a dividend under s. 263 of the Companies Act 1985 do not depend on a company producing a profit only in the current year.

54. Answer [D] is correct, purchase is out of capital, not a mere purchase. A company may purchase its own shares if it has power to do so under its articles ([C]). Table A, Article 35 confers this power. Usually shares must be purchased out of the proceeds of a fresh issue of shares or out of distributable profits as in [B] but under s. 171 of the Companies Act 1985 a private company may purchase its own shares out of capital provided it is authorised by a special resolution and a statutory declaration by the directors that the company can pay its debts for the next 12 months. [A] is incorrect because purchase of own shares out of capital is only permissible if the company is a private company.

55. Answer [B] is correct. The principles of maintenance of capital are intended to protect the creditors of a company. These principles are shown in statement i, ii and v and also in the prohibition on a company giving financial assistance for the purchase of its own shares and the rule that a company cannot hold shares in its holding company. The other statements, although concerned with the shares do not deal with the principle of maintenance of capital. Statement iv is s. 80 of the Companies Act 1985 — authorisation by the articles or by an ordinary resolution. A company may issue different classes of shares as in statement iii depending on how the company wishes to organise its capital structure. However, neither statement iii or iv relates to maintenance of capital.

56. Answer [A] is correct although [B], [C] and [D] are all true statements about the remedy of winding up on just and equitable grounds under s. 122(1)(g). Winding up is a drastic remedy and has the effect of ending the existence of the company. This may be the most appropriate remedy in situations which are quasi partnership companies, see, for example, *Ebrahami* v *Westbourne Galleries Limited* [1973] AC 360. In such situations it is probably preferable that the company ceases to exist as the members are no longer acting with cooperation and have no mutual trust or agreement. In other situations it may not give the desired result.

57. Answer [D] is correct. The test imposed for wrongful trading under s. 214 of the Insolvency Act 1986 is whether the director at some time before the commencement of the winding up of the company knew or ought to have concluded that there was no reasonable prospect that the company would avoid going into insolvent liquidation. Once that realisation has dawned the directors should take every step to minimize loss to the creditors. The fact that the other directors did not know about the company's difficult position is no defence because they should have asked for financial information if it was not given to them. Ned is therefore not guilty alone as in [A], [B] and [C].

58. Answer [C] is correct. The order of priority of payment of debts is fixed charge, costs of liquidation, preferential creditors, floating charge and finally unsecured creditors. Each class of creditor is paid off fully before moving down to the next class of creditors. If there is not enough money to pay off all the creditors in the class then each creditor receives an equal percentage payment. In this example Tom is an unsecured creditor. There is £20,000 left to pay off creditors totalling £60,000. Therefore all unsecured creditors will receive one-third of the money owed to them, giving Tom £1,000.

59. Answer [B] is correct. *Dawson International plc* v *Coats Patons plc* [1988] 4 BCC 305 is authority for the proposition that directors owe fiduciary duties to the company on a takeover (statements ii, iii and iv) and not to themselves as in statement i. One of the issues to consider is obviously the share price being offered (statement iii) and also the long-term prospects for the company (statement ii). Fiduciary duty to the company extends to the interests of the shareholders and employees of the company (statement iv).

60. Answer [D] is correct. The Cadbury Committee reported in 1992. The Report comprised a Code of Best Practice ('the Cadbury Code') to be adopted by the boards of directors of all listed companies. The requirement to comply with the Cadbury Code is now a continuing obligation of listing of the Stock Exchange. Central to the recommendations was the introduction of non-executive directors who were to bring an element of objectivity into the operation of the company. Statement i shows that the Code of Best Practice 1.2 allows the chairman and chief executive to be the same person with the proviso that no one person should have unfettered control. Statement ii shows that the remuneration committee should consist of non-executive directors. Statement iii is the opposite of the Cadbury recommendations. Statement iv is a key part of the Cadbury recommendations.

APPENDIX 4

NOTE-FORM ANSWERS TO MCT2

1. Answer [A] is correct. Allowing a company to issue shares in return for non-cash assets raises the danger that the shares might be credited as paid up to a value in excess of the value of the non-cash asset. To avoid this danger, ss. 103 and 108 of the Companies Act 1985 places strict rules of independent valuation on the asset. These rules have a prominent place in respect of public companies, whereas private companies appear to enjoy a more generous treatment (see *Re Wragg Ltd* [1897] 1 Ch 796). Exceptions to s. 103 do exist, even in respect of public companies and these can be found in propositions [B], [C] and [D]. [C] and [D] are important and reflect and permit take-over activity.

2. Answer [C] is correct. Companies do enjoy perpetual succession ([A]) and shareholders do enjoy limited liability ([B]) as opposed to the unlimited liability suffered by partners in a partnership. There currently exists no statutory requirement that independent directors are appointed ([D]) despite the calls from the Cadbury Committee and others (see the EC Fifth Draft Directive on Company Law), although some companies do appoint independent directors and report on their appointments. Proposition [C] reflects the need to protect investors and creditors through disclosure and returns. These requirements exist on the formation of a company through the need to present certain documents and statements before a Certificate of Incorporation is granted, and remain with a company throughout its life through the rules in respect of annual accounts, annual returns and directors' reports.

3. Answer [D] is correct. Elective resolutions were introduced by the Companies Act 1989 as part of the regime for the deregulation of private companies. The provisions are now found in ss. 379A, 381A, 381B and 382A of the Companies Act 1985. Essentially a written resolution signed by all members who are entitled to attend and vote at a meeting can reduce the administrative burden on the company by dispensing with the requirements to pass certain resolutions in respect of matters specified by the Secretary of State by statutory instrument. These include the requirements in respect of the laying of accounts and reports before a general meeting (s. 252 of the Companies Act 1985). Other matters that can form the basis of elections include, the dispensing with the holding of an annual general meeting (s. 366A of the Companies Act 1985) and with the annual appointment of creditors (s. 386 of the Companies Act). [A] demands a special resolution (s. 28 of the Companies Act 1985). [B] is subject to the requirements and details of the company's articles of association. Table A, Article 82, provides for matters to be dealt with by ordinary resolution. Dividends and distributions ([C]) combine a requirement that directors make a recommendation (s. 234 of the Companies Act 1985) but that the members in general meeting declare a dividend through the passing of an ordinary resolution (Table A, Article 102).

4. Answer [C] is correct. Section 80 of the Companies Act 1985 provides some broad controls on directors' abilities to issue and allot shares. Generally, the board enjoy the power to issue shares following the authority given to them via an ordinary resolution in general meeting or through authority given by a provision in the company's articles of association. A director who knowingly and wilfully contravenes, permits or authorises a contravention of s. 80 is liable to a fine (in this instance, Julian). However, the purchaser of those shares might be unaware of this position and is usually an innocent purchaser. Section 80 provides that an allotment of shares by directors without a proper authorisation is not invalid and the purchaser of the shares obtains good title; in this instance, Beryl as the purchaser obtains that good title.

5. Answer [D] is correct. The question focuses on the judicial treatment of groups. Statements [A] and [B] are too sweeping and fail accurately to reflect exceptions to the principles. [C] is too narrow. Although statutory provisions do exist requiring that in certain narrow instances groups of companies are treated as one entity, for example the need to produce consolidated accounts, the court can and has gone beyond the statutory provisions in order to recognise groups of companies. The most often cited instance of this is *DHN Food Distributors Ltd* v *Tower Hamlets London Borough Council* [1976] 1 WLR 852. However, doubts have been cast over the soundness of the Court of Appeal's decision in that case (see *Woolfson* v *Strathclyde Regional Council* 1978 SLT 159 and *Adams* v *Cape Industries plc* [1990] Ch 433). Nevertheless, the situation remains that the courts can pierce or lift the veil of incorporation in a group situation if persuaded that special circumstances exist indicating that it is a mere facade concealing the true facts. The identification and meaning of those special circumstances remains difficult and uncertain.

6. Answer [B] is correct. This is a question concerning the number of directors only, not the number of members where a single member private company is now permitted (s. 1 of the Companies Act 1985). [B] gives the correct advice. Section 282 of the Companies Act 1985 requires every public company to have at least 2 directors (unless it was registered before 1 November 1929) and every private company to have at least 1 director. [A] specifies the incorrect number. [D] and [C] are incorrect, in that the statutory minimum number is not satisfied and the issue of procedure and resolutions is irrelevant.

7. As this question is concerned with the minimum number of shareholders in a public limited company, the correct answer is [C] (s. 1 of the Companies Act 1985). [A] gives the wrong number of shareholders and so is incorrect. The position is different for private limited companies where the Companies (Single Member Private Limited Companies) Regulations 1992 (SI 1992 No. 1699) amended s. 1 of the Companies Act 1985 to permit private limited companies with 1 shareholder only. Section 24 of the Companies Act 1985 becomes relevant to Tom in that it opens up the opportunity for personal liability unless Tom was a single member of a private limited company. [D] and [B] are incorrect. [B] represents the pre-1992 position and [D] represents a pre-1980 position in respect of public limited companies only.

8. Answer [A] is correct. The question demanded knowledge of both the process of alteration via a special resolution (s. 9 of the Companies Act 1985) and the controls on that process and alteration. The controls are found in statute and at common law. The statutory controls are explained in s. 9. The common law controls have evolved and developed from a long line of cases and decisions. The classic statement and restriction that an alteration must be '*bona fide* for the benefit of the company as a whole' is to be found in the judgment of Lindley MR in *Allen* v *Gold Reefs of West Africa Ltd* [1900] 1 Ch 656 at 671–2. It has been accepted and developed in the subsequent cases, see *Greenhalgh* v *Arderne Cinemas Ltd* [1951] Ch 286. Although other methods of alteration do exist, for example, unanimous consent or by ordinary resolution pursuant to s. 80, none of these are represented in propositions [B], [C] or [D].

9. Answer [C] is correct. The question is concerned with members' rights and the statutory contract found in s. 14 of the Companies Act 1985. One result of the statutory contract is that members and the company must adhere to those provisions in the articles dealing with members' rights and obligations. This indicates, in this instance, an obligation on Robert to use arbitration in an attempt to settle his dispute with the company. His failure to do this is in breach of the s. 14 statutory contract. The case of *Hickman* v *Kent or Romney Marsh Sheep-Breeders' Association* [1915] 1 Ch 881, is of relevance in that on the basis of similar facts the court confirmed the status and effect of the statutory contract. [A] concerns circumstances when the veil may be lifted. [B] concerns early non-disclosure of negotiations being undertaken by directors. [D] concerns the non-entitlement to remuneration by directors.

10. [B] is the correct answer. This question concerns the ability of a company to alter its articles of association when that alteration results in the breach of a contract with a third person. In *Southern Foundries (1926) Ltd* v *Shirlaw* [1940] AC 701 it was able to exercise its statutory right to alter its articles of association despite the fact that the alteration itself might cause a breach of contract. The remedy of an injunction will not be available, but damages should be available to compensate for the breach of contract. Bert will not, therefore, be able to prevent the alteration and the breach, but he should be able to seek damages for the premature termination of his fixed term appointment. [A] concerns forgiveness of directors' negligence by a majority of members provided there has been no fraud on the minority. [C] concerns lifting the veil to expose a facade. [D] concerns managing directors.

11. Answer [D] is correct. This question concerns the trick area of the remuneration of promoters, promoters do not enjoy any automatic right to remuneration, even to recover preliminary expenses. Answers [B] and [C] are therefore incorrect. Nor can the existence of a provision in the articles of association provide the promoter with a right of remuneration. Such a provision also fails of itself to create a contract between the promoter and the company. [A] is therefore incorrect. [D] represents the accurate position of requiring that the promoter establishes a contractual claim through the existence of a binding contract with the company's contractual capacity before the company came into existence (*Re English & Colonial Produce Co.* [1906] 2 Ch 435).

12. Answer [D] is correct. This question concerns an aspect of the duties of promoters and their fiduciary position. Profit on the sale of property to the company can be enjoyed provided full disclosure of it made and approved of it is forthcoming from an independent board of directors or an independent body of shareholders. Hence proposition [C] is incorrect stipulating no disclosure at all. Propositions [A] and [B] are also incorrect because they do not consist of independent shareholder or independent directors. Proposition [D] represents disclosure to independent parties, particularly the need to disclose to independent shareholders through a prospectus or through listing particulars (*Lagunas Nitrate Co.* v *Lagunas Syndicate* [1899] 2 Ch 392; *Gluckstein* v *Barnes* [1900] AC 240).

13. Answer [C] is correct. Section 36C of the Companies Act 1985 was introduced as an attempt to remove the subtle distinction that had developed in common law allowing the promoter to escape liability provided he signed 'as agent' rather than 'on behalf of the company'. Compare *Kelner* v *Baxter and others* (1866) LR 2 CP 174 with *Newbourne* v *Sensolid (Great Britain) Ltd* [1954] 1 QB 45. [A] and [B] represent the 'old' common law position, whereas [D] is incorrect.

14. Answer [D] is correct. The Companies Act 1989 introduced the new s. 3A into the Companies Act 1985 with the aim of simplifying the objects of a general commercial company and reducing lengthy objects classes to one general provision which would provide that a commercial company could carry on any trade or business whatsoever and do all such things as are incidental to the carrying on of that trade or business. A company can be incorporated with this general commercial object, or it may amend its objects clause to adopt it. [C] is incorrect. A company's implied powers are limited to support its objects in that a company will only be granted such powers that are necessary to support its objects (*Attorney-General* v *Manchester Corporation* [1906] 1 Ch 643). [A] is subject to s. 28 of the 1985 Act and [B] to s. 4.

15. Answer [A] is correct. This question concerns the difficult and, at times, confusing area of distinguishing between objects and powers. The situation is made difficult by the practice of expressing both powers and objects in the objects clause and adopting an independent objects provision which might read:

> . . . each clause and sub-clause should be construed independently of, and should in no way be linked by, reference to any other clause or sub-clause, and that the objects set out in each clause and sub-clause were independent objects of the company. . . .

The courts have struggled with such a provision for a long time, until the Court of Appeal in *Re Introductions Ltd* [1970] Ch 199 sought to clarify the position and adopted answer [A]. The Court of Appeal construed the ability to borrow as a power, not an object. As a result the power could only be used to support an object but the power could not, of itself, constitute an object nor could it become an independent object through the use of an independent objects clause. [A] therefore represents the correct position. [B], [C] and [D] seek either to enhance the status or the effect of an independent objects clause or they simply ignore the substantive differences between an object and a power in terms of nature and purpose.

16. Answer [B] is correct. Under the s. 35(2) of the Companies Act 1985 shareholders are given the right to bring proceedings to refrain the doing of an *ultra vires* act. The situation is a little complicated in that no such proceedings may be brought in respect of any act which is to be done in fulfilment of a legal obligation arising from a previous act of the company. [A] contradicts [B] and is incorrect. [D] is incorrect in that companies can and do act *ultra vires* with differing consequences. [C] has no legal foundation, despite the vast practical powers of directors.

17. Answer [D] is correct. Section 35(3) of the Companies Act 1985 retains the common law position by providing that 'it remains a duty of the directors to observe any limitations on their powers flowing from the company's memorandum'. It also provides that the shareholders may by special resolution relieve directors from liability for failing to observe limits flowing from the company's memorandum. The need for a special resolution confirms that statement [C] is incorrect. [A] is also incorrect. Section 35(1) removes the possibility of claiming that an *ultra vires* contract is unenforceable. It also provides the basis for concluding that [B] is incorrect. The *ultra vires* contract can be enforced against the company.

18. Answer [C] is correct. This question concerns the difficult area of directors' authority. Although there exists a wealth of case law in this area, especially in relation to the principles of agency and authority, it is normal to focus on the recent statutory rules that have been developed. Section 35A(1) of the Companies Act 1985 provides that:

> In favour of a person dealing with a company in good faith, the power of the board of directors to bind the company, or to authorise others to do so, shall be deemed to be free of any limitation under the company's constitution.

Thus it appears that [C] is correct. Lost Limited must have acted in good faith albeit that the meaning of this is uncertain (see *International Sales & Agencies Ltd* v *Marcus* [1982] 3 All ER 551; *Barclays Bank Ltd* v *TOSG Trust Fund Ltd* [1984] BCLC 18). Section 35B appears to remove the duty to inquire, whilst s. 35(A)(2)(b) provides that even actual knowledge of any constitutional limits does not of itself amount to bad faith. Although it is clear from the wording of s. 35(A)(1) that bad faith will defeat a claim ([D]). Similarly the wording of s. 35(A)(1) is contrary to the suggestion that the contract can never be enforced ([A]) or can be enforced only with the company's agreement ([B]).

19. In order to answer this question, knowledge of s. 322A of the Companies Act 1985 is required. Section 322A essentially provides that where a director, or a connected person or associated company, is a party to a transaction it is voidable at the instance of the company and s. 35A does not apply. Thus [B] is correct. Despite

s. 35A and the good faith of the director, the contract is unauthorised and remains voidable at the option of the company. [C] is covered by s. 35A. [D] is incorrect in that an *intra vires* contract shall be valid and enforceable: see s. 35(1). [A] is now dealt with by s. 23(1) allowing the contract to be enforced.

20. Answer [C] is correct. The rule in *Turquand's* case was developed to reduce the severity of the constructive notice rule whereby outsiders were deemed to know the contents and requirements of documents registered at the Companies Registry. With the abolition of the constructive notice rule and the introduction of wide powers under ss. 35 and 35A of the Companies Act 1985, the importance of the *Turquand* rule has decreased. In many circumstances, where there exists an overlap *Turquand* is overridden by s. 35A. In others, for example, a decision taken by a body which purports to be the board of the company but which is improperly constituted, the rule in *Turquand* will prevail. [A], [B] and [D] do not represent the rule in *Turquand's* case, albeit [B] bears a strong resemblance to the application of s. 35A.

21. Answer [A] is correct. The issue of the tortious and criminal liability of a company has perplexed the courts for some time, particularly when concerned with the issue of identifying a company's directing mind. One of the leading cases on this issue is *Tesco Supermarkets Ltd* v *Nattrass* [1972] AC 153, where the House of Lords recognised that in appropriate circumstances a company would still enjoy a directing mind when delegating authority ([B]). This was followed by the Court of Appeal in *El Ajou* v *Dollar Land Holdings plc* [1994] BCC 143 ([C]) and by the House of Lords in *Re Supply of Ready Mixed Concrete (No. 2)* [1995] IAC 456 ([D]). The case of *Tett* v *Phoenix Property & Investment Co. Ltd* [1984] BCLC 599 is the odd one out (and therefore the correct answer) because it deals with the need to recognise that a company's power to refuse to register a transfer of shares is one which must be exercised *bona fide* for the benefit of the company.

22. Answer [D] is INCORRECT and therefore the right answer. Although a company is an 'entity' recognised as being subject to criminal law, exceptions recognise the unique nature of a company. [A] is correct in presuming a company cannot be connected in a crime that it is impossible for an artificial entity to perform, such as rape. Similarly, a company cannot serve a sentence of imprisonment ([B]). [C] is unusual but true. In *Richmond London Borough Council* v *Pinn & Wheeler Ltd* [1989] RTR 354, it was held that a company cannot be charged with an offence which involved the driving of a vehicle because of the required physical act of 'driving'. [D], therefore, is INCORRECT. Although a company and its directors of the same mind cannot constitute conspiracy, where a company and a person representing its directing mind were involved with other persons, at least two independent minds can be identified and the offence of conspiracy is possible (*R* v *IRC Holdings* [1944] 1 All ER 691).

23. Answer [C] is INCORRECT and therefore the right answer. Companies enjoy wide tortious liability including liability for the acts of their servants ([B]), strict liability ([A]) (*Lloyd* v *Grace Smith & Co.* [1912] AC 716) and liability where malice is required ([D]) enabling malice to be attributed to a company by proving that the company servant responsible for the commission of the tort behaved with malice whilst acting within the course of his employment (*Cornfield* v *Carlton Bank Ltd* [1899] 1 QB 392).

24. Answer [B] is correct. Generally, shareholders can hide behind nominees for purely personal reasons. However, a danger exists in that shareholders may wish to disguise a more sinister purpose, such as a take-over intention. To avoid this s. 198 of the Companies Act 1985 obliges a shareholder to notify the company concerned within 2 days of the acquisition of an interest in voting shares in a public company. An 'interest' normally means a holding of 3% in the shares of the company.

25. Answer [B] is INCORRECT and therefore the right answer. Although the details entered in the register of members are open to challenge in accordance with s. 359 of the Companies Act 1985 they cannot be challenged for any purpose. For example, in *Re Piccadilly Radio plc* [1989] BCLC 683, a court refused to correct an entry in the register because those seeking to rely on s. 359 were doing so not to benefit the company nor to protect their own membership interests, but rather to prevent the transfer of shares to a party opposed to a take-over bid in which the objectors were directly interested. The challenge was motivated by an ulterior, collateral purpose, and disallowed. Section 352, Companies Act 1985 supports [A], s. 22(1) Companies Act 1995 supports [C] and *Re Piccadilly Radio plc* supports [D].

26. Answer [B] is correct. The whole area of the transfer of shares and directors' rights of refusal is complex. Because we are dealing with a private limited company the matter is simplified in that refusal can only take place if the directors are empowered by the articles to do so. Usually the directors have absolute and unlimited discretion when exercising this power and are not bound to give reasons for refusing a transfer (*Berry and Stewart* v *Tottenham Hotspur Football & Athletic Co. Ltd* [1935] Ch 718). The court will not interfere with directors' exercise of such a power unless it is proved that they were not acting *bona fide* in the interests of the company (*Re Smith & Fawcett Ltd* [1942] Ch 304). [B] therefore represents the correct answer. Since directors do have rights [A] is not correct. There is no duty to give reasons ([C]). The type of share is irrelevant ([D]).

27. Answer [C] is correct. Section 89 of the Companies Act 1985 requires that before any equity shares are allotted they must first be offered to existing shareholders (pre-exemption rights). 'Equity' shareholding ([D]) includes ordinary ([A]) and preference ([B]) shares. Employee shares allow the workers in a company to participate in the profits they help create. Where shares are offered as an employee share scheme they are not subject to the general pre-exemption rules of the Companies Act.

28. Answer [C] is correct. People who invest in a company on the basis of a prospectus or listing particulars have the right to seek compensation if the prospectus or those particulars contain misleading information. However, a number of defences do exist. In respect of Blackwood plc, the defences can be found in s. 154A of the Financial Services Act 1986. These include [A], [B] and [D] but not [C]. [A], [B] and [C] defences are found in s. 157 (listed) or s. 154A (unlisted) of the Financial Services Act 1986. The requirement of reasonable belief on reasonable grounds includes a requirement that the belief was held at the time of issuing the prospectus and up to the time of allotment. If a change in the belief occurs between those two dates then a supplementary prospectus must be issued.

29. Answer [A] is correct. In *Bushell* v *Faith* [1970] 1 All ER 53 the articles of a company contained a clause which provided:

> In the event of a resolution being proposed at any general meeting of the company for the removal from office of any director, any shares held by that director shall on a poll in respect of such a resolution carry the right to three votes per share . . .

The effect of this clause was the defeat of any proposed resolution to remove a director. Nevertheless, the House of Lords accepted the provision on the grounds that it was not for the judiciary to interfere with a company's right to issue shares with special rights or restrictions. [B] concerns alteration of a company's articles. [C] concerns disqualification of directors and the test in s. 6 of the Companies Act 1985. [D] concerns individual directors pursuing a new venture on their own account after the board has concluded bona fide that the company shall not pursue it themselves.

30. Answer [C] is correct. Section 282 of the Companies Act 1985 provides that every public company must have at least 2 directors unless it was registered before 1 November 1929. No specific penalty exists for allowing the number of directors to fall below the statutory minimum. It is usual for a company to adopt Table A, Article 64 which provides that the company must have at least 2 directors unless the company determines otherwise by ordinary resolution. The same Article permits the company, by ordinary resolution, to set a maximum number of directors. Private limited companies are permitted to specify a minimum of 1 director only.

31. Answer [A] is correct. At one stage it was quite common for a company to specify a minimum shareholding qualification for its directors. This was permitted and was expected to encourage loyalty and commitment to the company. Although this is permitted, there does not exist any statutory requirement that directors must also be shareholders. [B] and [D] are therefore incorrect. Nor is there any requirement that a time period of 6 months is permitted for acquisition ([C]). The matter is normally dealt with by the articles of association, but s. 291 of the Companies Act 1985 applies when articles specify a share qualification requirement. Section 291 provides that directors must acquire the minimum shareholding within 2 months after appointment, or such shorter time as many be fixed by the articles, and that the office of any director not acquiring his qualifications within such time, or ceasing to hold it after such time, shall be vacated, and that the disqualified person shall not be capable of reappointment as director until he has obtained his qualification. Thus [A] is an accurate representation of the position of Tom.

32. Answer [C] is INCORRECT and therefore the right answer. This question focuses on the complex area of directors' remuneration. The starting point is the recognition that directors are not entitled as of right to any remuneration ([A]). It was established at a very early date that directors are not servants of the company and do not enjoy any implied right to remuneration (*Hutton* v *West Cork Railway Co.* (1883) 23 ChD 654). To overcome this principle it is common for the articles of association to provide for the remuneration of directors ([B]) or for directors to be appointed under service contracts as employees of the company with an accompanying right for payment. However, not all directors are appointed under service contracts and are caught by the general principle of no entitlement to remuneration. Thus [C], that all directors are employed under service contracts, is INCORRECT. Should a director be employed under a service contract and then act in excess of the requirements of that contract then [D] represents the correct position of a claim for *quantum meruit*.

33. Answer [A] is correct. The relationship between the board and the general meeting has been in a state of confusion in respect of the general meeting's right to interfere with decision of the board. Article 80 of Table A of the Companies Act 1948 seems to permit interference but confusion remains as to the form of that interference (see Sullivan (1977) 93 LQR 569). Article 70 of Table A in the Companies Act 1985 suggests that interference must be by special resolution cutting across these developments and the debate surrounding them. It was assumed that in certain situations of a failure to act by the board then the right to manage must revert back to the general meeting. This residual power of management is illustrated by the decision in *Barron* v *Potter* [1914] 1 Ch 895 where a company had two directors who were given the power to appoint additional directors. The company's business came to a halt because one of the directors refused to attend any board meetings at which the other was present. The court explained that in the situation of deadlock, where the directors were unwilling to appoint additional directors under the power conferred on them by the articles, the company in general meeting shall have the power to make the appointment. [B] concerns the s. 14 of the Companies Act 1985 contract. [C] involves notice of board meetings to directors. [D] concerns maladministration of shareholders' meetings.

34. [B] is INCORRECT and therefore the right answer. Perhaps surprisingly, the general law is that the directors cannot appoint one of themselves to an office of profit or delegate power to a managing director unless expressly empowered to do so by the articles or by a resolution of the company (see *Nelson* v *James Nelson & Sons Ltd* [1914] 2 KB 770 and answer [A]), although principles of agency will recognise the general powers of a managing director (see *Freeman & Lockyer* v *Buckhurst Park Properties (Mangal) Ltd and another* [1964] 2 QB 480 and answer [D]). Most companies enjoy the power to appoint a managing director through Article 84 of Table A, with the ability to delegate powers through Article 72 of Table A. The power to remove a director by ordinary resolution under s. 303 of the Companies Act 1985 remains despite a director's appointment to the position of managing director ([C]).

35. Answer [D] is correct. Every company must have a company secretary who enjoys extensive duties and responsibilities. The company secretary is an officer of the company and enjoys express and implied powers to bind the company on contracts in respect of the administrative matters of the company. For example, in *Panorama Developments (Guildford) Ltd* v *Fidelis Furnishing Fabrics Ltd* [1971] 2 QB 711, a company was bound under a contract to hire cars. The contract was entered into by the company secretary on behalf of the company, but the cars were used for the secretary's own purposes and not by the company. Nevertheless, the Court of Appeal held that the company secretary had apparent or ostensible authority to enter into contracts connected with the administrative side of the company's affairs, including the hiring of cars. Because the company secretary enjoys powers to order goods [A] is not correct, and because these powers are extensive, [B] and [C] are not correct.

36. Answer [B] is correct. Statutory controls exist on the length and terms of contracts of employment made with directors. Generally, a company should enjoy the right to remove a director upon giving reasonable notice and without the need to pay large sums in compensation for premature termination of the contract; unless, of course, the company wishes to place itself in that position. Hence, s. 319 of the Companies Act 1985 provides that terms of protection in contracts for 5 years or more are void unless approved in advance by the member in general meeting. It is the terms, not the contract itself, that is void. Thus [B] is correct not [A]. [C] and [D] are also incorrect in that no general power of approval is granted to the general meeting of members.

37. Answer [A] is correct. The Company Directors Disqualification Act 1986 provides the grounds for the disqualification of a director or others. Many of the grounds are discretionary, hence we need to identify likely and probable grounds for disqualification. [B], [C] and [D] are all specifically mentioned in the Act as grounds for disqualification and therefore provide a possibility and a likelihood of disqualification. [A] is not specifically mentioned in the Act and, although the Act does contain a right to disqualify on the broad category of 'unfitness', it is UNLIKELY to include cases of commercial misjudgement as opposed to conduct that is dishonest or in breach of standards of commercial misjudgment or is grossly incompetent (see *Re Lo-Line Electric Motors Ltd* [1988] Ch 477).

38. Answer [D] is correct. In *Industrial Development Consultants v Cooley* [1972] 2 All ER 162 a managing director of a company failed to secure a valuable contract for the company to do work for a local gas board. He then secured the contract in his personal and private capacity but was held liable to account to the company for the profit which he obtained from performing the contract. Directors are subject to fiduciary duties and principles including the broad principle that they must avoid a conflict of interest and duty. Both Sandra, in our question, and the managing director in *Industrial Development Consultants v Cooley* have allowed their personal interest to conflict with their duties as directors. Conflicts must be disclosed and approved. [A] concerns maladministration of a shareholders' meeting. In [B] the alteration of the articles of association was valid. In [C] persons gathering without notice of a shareholders' meeting must consent to the gathering being considered a meeting of members.

39. Answer [B] is correct. [A], [C] and [D] all represent actual duties of directors. [A] and [D] emanate from the common law following a long line of established cases. [C] follows the recommendations of the Committee of Inquiry on Industrial Democracy (the Bullock Report (Cmnd 6706, 1977) and has been enacted in s. 309 of the Companies Act 1985. There is no general requirement that directors should be under a duty to consider the interests of their fellow directors or of the board collectively [B].

40. Answer [A] is correct. A complex collection of rules and exceptions apply to loans and related transactions. [B], [C] and [D] fall within the exceptions. [B] is covered by s. 334 of the Companies Act 1985 which exempts entirely loans made to a director of the company or of its holding company if the aggregate of such loans outstanding does not exceed £5,000. Under s. 337 a company can provide disclosed and approved loans or funds to directors to enable them to meet expenditure to be incurred for the purposes of their duties, subject to a £20,000 ceiling in respect of relevant companies ([C]). Section 338 provides that money lending companies can make loans to directors provided they are made on the ordinary terms of the business ([D]) and not on favourable terms ([A]).

41. Answer [C] is correct. All the others represent actual requirements of s. 56 of the Criminal Justice Act 1993. [C] is not a requirement in that it refers to securities or issuers in GENERAL, whereas s. 56 requires the information to relate to particular securities or to a particular issuer, or particular issuers, of securities. A classic example of information relating to a particular issuer is a decision to make a take-over bid for that issuer.

42. Answer [C] is correct. Although [C] is similar in content to [D], [D] adds a requirement of belief on 'reasonable grounds'. Unlike the defences to the dealing and encouragement offences where 'reasonable grounds' is a requirement, no such requirement is expected in respect of the defence of the offence of disclosing information (see s. 53 of the Criminal Justice Act 1993). [A] and [B] are also excluded as they are omitted from s. 53 as providing defence to the disclosure offence.

43. Answer [D] is the correct solution. This refers to an identifiable corporate asset which is usually the subject of a fixed charge. The fact that the property is future property is irrelevant (*Re Yorkshire*

Woolcombers Association Ltd [1903] 2 Ch 284). The other characteristics ([A], [B] and [C]) are those identified by Romer LJ in the same case, as characteristics of floating charges.

44.   Answer [B] is correct. Under s. 395 of the Companies Act 1985 a company is obliged to register a charge with the Registrar within 21 days after the date of its creation. Under ss. 399(3) and 400(4) failure to effect registration of a charge renders the company, and every officer in default, liable to a fine. [A] and [D] appear to confine the fine to a company or its officers only and are incorrect. [C] refers to civil action only and although this might be a possibility, it is not the only action available.

45.   Answer [C] is the correct solution. Section 399 of the Companies Act 1985 confirms propositions [A] and [B] ensuring that the charge is void. Similarly it is accepted that the void charge does not give any priority or preferences over other creditors ([D]). Despite the 'void' status of the charge, the loan remains repayable. The charge merely affects the security and priority status. Hence [C] is NOT a consequence of a failure to register the charge. Section 407 of the Companies Act 1985 goes a stage further and declares that 'if a charge becomes void to any extent then the whole of the sum secured by the charge is payable forthwith on demand'.

46.   Answer [D] is the correct solution. Section 245 of the Insolvency Act 1986 is intended to prevent an unsecured creditor of a company obtaining a floating charge to secure his existing debt and thus gain an advantage over other unsecured creditors. It enables a liquidator of a company to call in question floating charges created by the company in a certain period before the commencement of the winding up. In respect of a person connected with the company, including shadow directors ([C]), the liquidator can challenge charges created up to 2 years prior to the commencement of the winding up – irrespective of the financial position of the company at the date of granting the charge. In respect of non-connected persons, the relevant time period is 12 months prior to the commencement of the winding-up, but here it must be shown that the company was unable to pay its debts when it gave the charge or became unable to do so 'in consequence of the transaction under which the share is created' ([A] or [B]). Under [D] this final requirement remains unsatisfied.

47. Answer [A] is the correct advice. Generally, companies are not permitted to purchase their own shares (s. 143, Companies Act 1985). Exceptions to this harsh rule exist provided a company is authorised to do so by its articles and provided the company complies with the relevant statutory purchase procedures. In most instances the company will be obliged to purchase the shares out of the proceeds of a fresh issue or out of available distributable profits but this is not the only source of funds ([B]). Private companies, such as Glass Ltd, are permitted access to their capital to fund the purchase of shares in so far as the company's distributable profits are of an insufficient value to facilitate the purchase (s. 171 of the Companies Act 1985). The expenditure taken from capital is referred to as 'the permissible capital payment'. The courts are not obliged to authorise this payment ([C]) but s. 164(2) requires the members to pass a special resolution authorising the expenditure ([A]).

48. Answer [C] is correct. The question concerns the very difficult area of understanding the exemptions to s. 151 of the Companies Act 1985. In particular it concerns the exemption in s. 153(1) where a company is permitted to give financial assistance for the purchase of shares where the company's principal purpose in providing assistance was not aimed at facilitating the acquisition of shares, or the giving of the assistance for the acquisition was but an incidental part of some larger purpose. Similarly, s. 153(2) provides an exception where the company's principal purpose in giving assistance was not to reduce or discharge any liability incurred by a person for the purpose of the acquisition of shares in the company or its holding company, or the reduction or discharge of any such liability was but an incidental part of some larger purpose of the company. In respect of both of these exceptions a larger purpose is permitted; however, following the decision in *Brady* v *Brady* [1989] AC 755 their scope has been severely restricted. *Brady* v *Brady* involved a restructuring scheme in a situation of conflict and deadlock. In a rather restrictive interpretation, Lord Oliver explained that the mischief against which s. 151 was aimed must always be borne in mind and that a distinction must be drawn between a purpose and the reason for that purpose. If the purpose was to provide assistance, the reason being part of a reorganisation, that reason was not part of a larger purpose – the purpose remains that of prohibited assistance for purchase ([C]). It is this reasoning and its consequence that have inspired Department of Trade and Industry proposals for reform in this area. The decision in *Brady* v *Brady* does not illustrate propositions [A] and [B], both of which are covered by specific statutory provisions: ss. 263 and 151 of the Companies Act 1985. [D] is directly contrary to that illustrated in *Brady* v *Brady*. As Lord Oliver indicated above, the courts are not prepared to accept primary and secondary purposes as the one purpose for the expenditure, a distinction will always be maintained.

49. Answer [C] is correct. The rule in *Foss* v *Harbottle* (1843) 2 Hare 461 exists to respect the majority rule principle, i.e. that the wishes of the majority of shareholders should prevail. This is opposite to the proposition that the wishes of the majority of directors should prevail ([D]). The practical consequence of the rule is therefore reflected in [C] in that it is for the company to sue for wrongs committed against it, not for individual shareholders to sue save in a few exceptional circumstances (*Percival* v *Wright* [1902] 2 Ch 421). Other aspects of the role in *Foss* v *Harbottle* reflect the 'internal management' principle and the 'irregularity' principle. The irregularity principle expects the company to resolve irregularities (contrary to [A]); the 'internal management' principle reflects the proposition that the courts will not interfere with the internal management of companies acting within their powers ([B]).

50. Answer [B] is correct. The decision in *Brown* v *La Trinida* (1887) 37 ChD 1 is often used to illustrate the irregularity principle. The case involved a minor irregularity in giving inadequate notice of a directors' meeting at which a motion to remove one of the directors was passed. The issue of inadequate notice was not sufficient to cause the courts to overturn the resolution. *Daniels* v *Daniels* [1978] Ch 406 ([A]) illustrates that a negligent misappropriation of corporate assets can constitute 'fraud' on the minority. Similarly, *Estmanco (Kilner House) Ltd* v *Greater London Council* [1982] 1 All ER 437 ([C]), illustrates that gaining an unfair advantage might constitute fraud; whereas, in *Cook* v *Deeks and others* [1916] 1 AC 554 ([D]) an intentional misappropriation of corporate assets constituted fraud.

51. Answer [A] is correct. For some time concerns existed as to whether the unfairly prejudiced conduct should be shown to be confined to part of the membership only or should be allowed even if it applied equally to all members of the company. The original wording of s. 459 did not assist here (see *Re a Company (No. 00370* *of 1987)* [1988] 1 WLR 1068). As a result of the Companies Act 1989, an amendment was introduced with the result that a petition under s. 459 may now be commenced irrespective of whether unfairly prejudiced conduct affects a part of the membership or the members generally. Although [B] is correct to the extent that it confirms interests to member interests and not personal and private interests (as per [D]) it is incorrect in insisting that the contract affects part only of the membership. Neither criminal intent nor malice are requirements of s. 459 ([C] and [D]).

52. Answer [D] is correct. The issue of disqualification is one dealt with under the Company Directors Disqualification Act 1986, not through s. 461(2) of the Companies Act 1985. [A], [B] and [C] are specifically mentioned in s. 461(2) but they do not detract from nor replace the general discretionary power given to the courts by s. 461 to make any order it thinks fit.

53. Answer [D] is correct. [A], [B] and [C] have been adopted by later courts as guidance in the application of s. 122(1)(g) of the Insolvency Act 1986 and the wide discretion given to the courts to determine when it is 'just and equitable' to order the winding up of a company. The facts of *Ebrahimi* v *Westbourne Galleries* [1973] AC 360 support and illustrate their application, where a special underlying obligation existed when a partnership was converted to a private company but one of the original partners was subsequently removed from his position as a director of the company with the result that he no longer participated in the management of the company and no longer received any remuneration. [D] was NOT included in Lord Wilberforce's suggestions, nor is s. 122(1)(g) confined to private companies. The issue of substratum and main object was present in *Re German Date Coffee Co.* (1882) 20 ChD 169.

54. Answer [A] is correct. All the other propositions represent resolutions identified in s. 84(1) of the Insolvency Act 1986. Generally, a company will adopt a special resolution [B] but in exceptional circumstances [C] and [D] will be available. It should be noted that the exceptional circumstances are those specified, i.e. where the company is unable to pay its debts ([C]) or a certain event or time has been reached as specified in the company's articles of association ([D]). Normally, [C] will be irrelevant because the circumstances are such that one would expect a creditors' voluntary winding up to have commenced. If members are dissatisfied with management ([A]) it is normal to use an ordinary resolution to remove each director (Companies Act 1985, s. 303). Winding up is possible, but normally a special resolution of the members will be required.

55. Answer [D] is correct. This question concerns the area of corporate insolvency and the ability to render directors personally liable for corporate debts – or at least make them contribute to funds during insolvency. Section 214 of the Insolvency Act 1986 concerns wrongful trading and applies to directors who allow a company to continue to trade at a time when they know or ought to have concluded that there was no reasonable prospect of the company avoiding insolvency. From the facts given, this would seem to apply to Ian. Section 212 of the Insolvency Act 1986 applies in misfeasance proceedings with the result that liable persons will be obliged to contribute to a company's assets in the course of a winding-up in respect of a breach of a fiduciary duty or a duty of care. Ian in directing business away from Holmes plc appears to be in breach of such a duty omitted from answer [A]. Section 213 of the Insolvency Act 1986 deals with fraudulent trading of which there is no evidence on the facts presented and is therefore inapplicable and irrelevant.

56. Answer [C] is correct. Although it might be a matter of concern that the company is not achieving its objects, that of itself does not constitute a ground for the Secretary of State to use the discretion available and order an investigation of the company's affairs. [A], [B] and [D] are all included in s. 432(2) as grounds for the exercise of the discretion. Of course, under s. 432(1) no discretion is involved when the court declares that a company's affairs should be investigated: the Secretary of State must appoint inspectors when ordered to do so by the court.

57. The advice in [D] represents the correct solution. The question involves the application of the detailed rules in the Companies Act 1985, part XIIIA. These notes deal with the compulsory acquisition of minority shareholding and normally involve giving to the offeror the right to purchase remaining shareholder interests once the offerors' offer has been accepted by 90% of shareholders, generally or in a particular class. However, the situation involving Tom and Jet Ltd is the reverse: it involves a member wishing to leave upon discovering that 90% of shareholding will be in the hands of Jet Ltd. The Companies Act provides for this situation. Section 430A(1) and (2) provide that if the 90% limit is reached, then a shareholder who has not accepted the offer can require the offeror to acquire his shares, and the offeror is bound to acquire the shares on the terms of the offer or on such other terms as may be agreed (s. 430B(2)). Thus the advice in [D] is accurate, although [C] does come close. However, [C] refers to a fresh offer whereas the legislation refers to the 'terms of the original offer'. [A] is not appropriate nor is [B] as this relates to Wing Ltd only.

58. Answer [B] is correct. [A], [C] and [D] are exceptions to the definition of a distribution (s. 263(2)(c), (a) and (b), respectively). Although it is normal to refer to dividends as distributors, distributions and the rules attached to such distributions apply to a much wider form of return. The circumstances in [B] involve a distribution, or a return in the form of the undervalue placed on the asset. It is similar in detail to the facts in *Aveling Barford Ltd v Perion Ltd* (1989) 5 BCC 677, where a sale at an undervalue of an asset of Aveling Barford Ltd to another company controlled by the sole beneficial shareholder of Aveling Barford Ltd was held to be a distribution to him.

59. Answer [C] is correct. Although the City Code is voluntary in nature, some parties may not like the application or interpretation of the Code. There exists a right of appeal against a decision of the City Panel to the Appeal Committee of the Panel. From that, an aggrieved party might be able to seek judicial review of the decision (contrary to [A]). The problem with the availability of judicial review is that it creates delay, uncertainty and could be applied for as part of a delaying tactic in the hope that a party will forgo the merger or takeover. In *R v Panel on Takeovers and Mergers, ex parte Datafin plc* [1987] QB 815, the court recognised the problems of permitting judicial review of the decisions of the panel but indicated that judicial review will be available but subject to the safeguards that it will be subject to the leave of the court, which would be given sparingly, and that the tendency would be to give declarations as the future meaning and applications of rules rather than the actual reversing of the decision under consideration. Since the courts are unwilling to overrule the City Panel, [B] and [D] are therefore incorrect.

60. Answer [A] is correct. The City Code on Takeover and Mergers, issued by the Panel on Takeovers and Mergers, represents the collective opinion of those professionally involved in the field of takeovers as to good business standards and as to how fairness to shareholders can be achieved. It consists of a voluntary code of rules and principles. It is not statutory based ([B]), nor does it confine itself to legal rights attaching to shares ([D]) although it does seem to ensure the fair and equal treatment of shareholders – not necessarily a consideration of their legal rights. Competition issues in respect of takeovers and mergers are dealt with through legislation not through the City Panel ([C]).

TITLES IN THE SERIES